Dresden: Treasures from the Saxon State Library

CIRCULUS
SAXONIÆ SUPERIORIS
in quo
DUCATUS & ELECTORATUS SAXONIÆ
MARCHIONATUS MISNIÆ
et
LANDGRAVIATUS THURINGIÆ
cum insertis et finitimis Regionibus exhibentur
à
IOHANNE BAPTISTA HOMANNO
Norimbergæ
CHURF und HERZOGTHUMS SAXEN
MEISSNER GEBIET
MEISSEN
MARGGRAFSCHAFT
ERTZGEBURG
BÖHMEN
WITTENBERG
TORGAW
LEIPZIG
MEISSEN
DRESDEN
ZWICKAW
PLAWEN
ALTENBURG
HALL

Dresden

Treasures *from the* Saxon State Library

Edited by

Margrit B. Krewson

The Publishing Office would like to acknowledge the editorial assistance of Allison Blakely, Ingrid M. Maar, Lys Ann Shore, and Diane C. Stuart in the development of this catalog.

Design: Garruba|Dennis|Konetzka, Washington, DC.

Library of Congress Cataloging-in-Publication Data

Dresden: treasures from the Saxon State Library/edited by Margrit B. Krewson.

p. cm.
Catalog and essays to accompany the exhibit:
Dresden: treasures from the Saxon State Library.
Includes bibliographical references (p. 43).

Contents:
The history of the Saxon State Library/Wolfgang Frühauf—
Political ambition versus cultural commitment/Reinhardt Eigenwill—
The Protestant reformation in Saxony/Christian Zühlke—
The literature of romanticism in Dresden/Jans-Jürgen Sarfert—
Music in Saxony/Ortrun Landmann—
Illustrations.

ISBN 0-8444-0925-1 (acid free paper)
Copy 3 Z663 .D74 1996

1. Saxony (Germany)—Civilization—Exhibitions.
2. Saxony (Germany)—Civilization—Bibliography—Exhibitions.
3. Sächsische Landesbibliothek (Dresden, Germany)—Exhibitions.
4. Rare books—Germany—Dresden—Bibliography—Exhibitions.
5. Manuscripts—Germany—Dresden—Exhibitions.
6. Music—Germany—Dresden—Bibliography—Exhibitions.
7. Saxony (Germany)—Civilization—Sources—Exhibitions.
8. Dresden (Germany)—Civilization—Sources—Exhibitions.
I. Krewson, Margrit B. (Margrit Beran)
II. Sächsische Landesbibliothek (Dresden, Germany)
III. Library of Congress.

DD801.S347D74 1996
016.9431'8—dc20

96-2673
CIP

Contents

Foreword

The Library of Congress has recently sponsored exhibitions highlighting treasures from two of the world's major libraries: the Vatican Library in Rome and the Bibliothèque Nationale de France in Paris. Now, the Library is privileged to display treasures from the Saxon State Library (Sächsische Landesbibliothek) in Dresden, Germany.

Located on the Elbe River in central Europe, Dresden was founded in the thirteenth century. It was the seat of the Saxon rulers beginning in the fifteenth century and is currently the capital of the German Free State of Saxony. Because of its pivotal role in the late Renaissance and the Protestant Reformation in Germany, Dresden is known as the German Florence or the Florence of the North.

During the first half of the eighteenth century, under the rulers August I (Augustus the Strong) and his son August II, Saxony reached the pinnacle of its cultural influence, manifested in the spectacular baroque architecture of the capital city. Dresden became a major European cultural center, where monarchs fostered the arts and made significant additions to the city's art, museum, and library collections, which attracted many European travelers.

One of Dresden's outstanding cultural institutions is the Saxon State Library, which is now celebrating its four hundred fortieth anniversary. The Library of Congress is pleased to collaborate with the Saxon State Library to display a selection of its treasures. These collections were unavailable and largely unknown to two generations of Americans, since Dresden fell within the former Soviet bloc after 1945. The idea for this exhibition originated in 1992, shortly after the collapse of communism, when I had the opportunity to visit the Saxon State Library.

In 1978 the National Gallery of Art mounted an exhibition, "The Splendor of Dresden," emphasizing the magnificent art treasures of Saxony. The present exhibition focuses for the first time on Saxony's equally rich and valuable literary heritage. Displayed here are examples from the full range of treasures in the Saxon State Library—manuscripts, incunabula, books, music manuscripts, photographs, maps, and paintings—forming an anthology from the High Middle Ages through the nineteenth century.

The exhibition and this accompanying catalog are the result of four years of collaboration and planning between the Saxon State Library and the Library of Congress. I would especially like to acknowledge the efforts of Margrit B. Krewson, the Library's German/Dutch area specialist, for her organizational skills as well as her initiative in raising the necessary funds to make the exhibition and catalog possible.

The Library of Congress displays these treasures from the Saxon State Library as part of its mission to make the resources of the world's more readily known to the American public. We are indeed privileged with the loan of these treasures from Dresden, most of which have never been exhibited outside the Saxon State Library. We are pleased to be able thus to call attention to the rich European heritage preserved in Dresden.

James H. Billington
The Librarian of Congress

Editor's Preface

This catalog, which accompanies the exhibit "Dresden: Treasures from the Saxon State Library," is presented to the American public as an introduction to the rich literary, musical, and religious history of Dresden collections and libraries. A series of essays written by the professional staff of the Saxon State Library (Sächsische Landesbibliothek) includes a history of the Saxon State Library from its beginnings as a court library to its current role as the state library of Saxony and one of the preeminent libraries in Germany (Wolfgang Frühauf); an overview of the history of Saxony, with particular emphasis on the ruling Wettin family and its political and cultural ambitions (Reinhardt Eigenwill); an explanation of the origin and role of the Protestant Reformation in Saxony (Christian Zühlke); a discussion of the role of Dresden in the development of literature during the Romantic period at the beginning of the nineteenth century (Hans-Jürgen Sarfert); and an account of the rich musical heritage of Saxony, much of which is preserved in the Saxon State Library (Ortrun Landmann).

This exhibit could not have been realized without the support of Suzanne Thorin and the scholarly guidance of Prosser Gifford. In addition, I would like to acknowledge the professional and cooperative spirit of Wolfgang Frühauf, Saxon State Library.

Particularly noteworthy is the scholarly selection of objects for this exhibit under the direction of Manfred Mühlner, also of the Saxon State Library, with the assistance of Valentin Weber and Katrin Nitzschke of his staff. Photographic preparation for this catalog was done by Regine Richter.

The essays were translated with the assistance of Mary Pajic and edited with the assistance of Lisa M. Hisel. My sincere thanks for their generous and able support.

This catalog also includes forty illustrations chosen from the 189 items on display. Matthew Caulfield provided invaluable assistance with subject review for the captions, which were translated with the assistance of Ronald Bachman, Christina Connelly, Christian Hennig and staff, Inge Wolfe, and David Kraus, and edited with the able assistance of Ursula Lange. I thank them for lending their expertise to this project.

A bibliography of titles in English and German will guide those who wish to explore further the themes of the catalog and exhibit. The bibliography was compiled by Eberhard Stimmel of the Saxon State Library.

The exhibition and catalog were funded through the generous support of the Dresden Hilton Hotel, the Donors' Association for the Promotion of Sciences and Humanities in Germany, Kulturstiftung Dresden der Dresdner Bank (Dresden Cultural Foundation of the Dresdner Bank), Gesellschaft der Freunde und Förderer der Sächsischen Landesbibliothek (Friends of the Saxon State Library), the Saxon State Government, and the Federal Republic of Germany.

Margrit B. Krewson
Library of Congress
April 1996

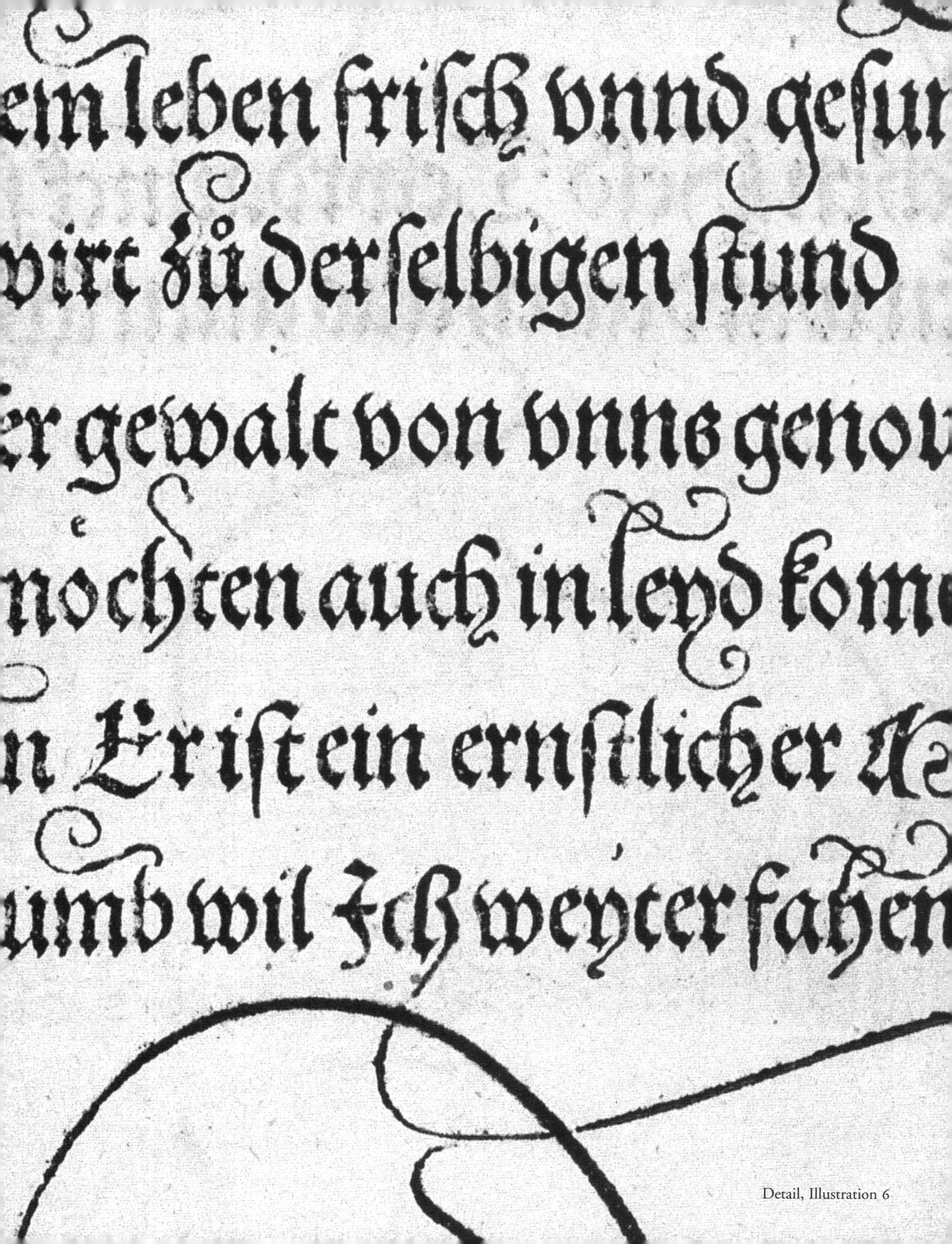

ein leben frisch vnnd gesun

wirt zů derselbigen stund

er gewalt von vnns genow

nochten auch in leyd kome

n Er ist ein ernstlicher M

umb wil Ich weyter fahen

Detail, Illustration 6

Wolfgang Frühauf

The History of the Saxon State Library

The Saxon State Library, the Sächsische Landesbibliothek, had its origins in the mid-sixteenth century, during the reign of Prince Elector August (ruled 1553–86). At that time, Saxony was the second-largest German state after the powerful Habsburg Empire, a position resulting primarily from the shrewd policies pursued by its princes and its great mineral wealth. Prince August, who lacked great military ambitions, concentrated his statesmanship on promoting the economy—especially mining, trade, agriculture, and forestry—and fostering the arts and sciences. This well-educated prince found his learned books becoming more and more indispensable, and in 1556 he began to acquire literary works systematically. This was the beginning of the Dresden Court Library.

The Private Library of the Prince Elector of Saxony

The new collection grew quite rapidly as Prince August personally perused the catalogs from the Leipzig book fair, went abroad on acquisition trips, and even commissioned diplomats to buy books for him. His love of books is illustrated not only by his meticulous selections but also by the splendid bindings he obtained from the atelier of Jakob Krause, the most important German bookbinder during the Renaissance. Prince August summoned Krause to Dresden from Augsburg, where the bookbinder had already demonstrated his mastery of the trade at the court of the Fuggers, a wealthy dynasty of merchant princes. The bindings Krause made for Prince August, partially made of white parchment and pigskin or costly calfskin, bore the coat of arms, insignia, and often the portrait of this Renaissance prince.

When Prince August died in 1586, he left behind a well-balanced library that included a collection of modern and foreign literature. As a collector, he was most interested in modern printed works. He also collected manuscripts, incunabula, and maps. None of these treasures originated from Saxon monasteries, which had once been the only centers of book learning in Saxony. When the monasteries were dissolved after the introduction of Protestantism as the official state religion in the first half of the sixteenth century, the University of Leipzig (founded 1409), was the chief beneficiary, although some Saxon private schools also received books from the monasteries. Instead, Prince August's acquisitions were mostly purchased. Next to each other on his bookshelves stood Catholic and Lutheran writings, although Calvinist books, partly because of their authors and partly because of their "erroneous doctrines," were kept elsewhere—just one indication of the religious troubles of the time. The dismissal of the librarian Leonhard, accused of being a Calvinist, offers another illustration of religious conflict in Saxony.

By the end of the sixteenth century, the electors, who followed one another in rapid succession, were no longer personally selecting books, and the library became the responsibility of the senior court chaplains. By 1595 the collection numbered 5,668 monographs and 91 maps and copper engravings. After this date the library's growth slowed markedly because of the Thirty Years' War, which brought rising prices, misery, and plague.

During the splendid reign of Johann Georg II (ruled 1656–80) conditions in the library improved. For the first time the electoral household and the court chaplains, as well as the elector's family, had access to the private library, though the household and chaplains could use it only by permission of the elector. This was the first step toward establishment of a public library.

The Golden Age

In the eighteenth century the collection flourished, becoming the preeminent German library. This golden age began with the reign of Prince Friedrich August I (ruled 1694–1733), who also became king of Poland in 1697 and who is generally known as August the Strong.

The new era had an inauspicious start with the burning of the residential palace in Dresden in 1701. Because of the damage to the castle, the library and other collections had to be moved to new, cramped quarters. King August summoned to his court talented architects, artists, craftsmen, and inventors, among them the "gold maker," Johann Friedrich Böttger, the creator of European porcelain. He also established numerous factories, which led to economic growth and made the court at Dresden the most splendid in Europe, after Versailles. He further expanded the royal collections, which he caused to be arranged by subject and made accessible to the public for the first time.

Thanks to increased financial support, the library was transformed. Manuscripts, maps, and valuable prints from other parts of the collection were added to it, and by 1727 it received additional space in two wings of the Zwinger. This collection of buildings, which is universally considered to be the best example of Dresden baroque architecture, was conceived as a court festival ground with an orangery, fountains, covered walks, and dining rooms.

The library had received many new acquisitions even before its move to the Zwinger, and the cataloging and use of the collections had expanded. Saxony was reveling in bibliophilia at that time, and literary history and bibliography had become fashionable. Book publishing and collecting had reached their zenith. Court and state officials rapidly built magnificent book collections, with the wealthy bourgeoisie trailing only slightly behind the nobility. The Court Library later purchased many of these private collections, some of the most important of which greatly raised its prestige. For example, in 1736, under the successor to August the Strong, Prince Friedrich August II (ruled 1733–63), the library acquired the collection of Johann von Besser (1654–1729), a poet and high court official. This collection of 18,000 volumes was especially strong in politics, history, and court ceremony and included objets d'art and curiosities, which were very popular in private libraries of the era.

An extremely rare item was added to the library in 1734. Johann Christian Götze, a court chaplain who had been appointed chief inspector of the Court Library, acquired an illustrated manuscript on a trip to Vienna: one of only three extant Maya manuscripts. Today the *Codex Dresdensis,* as it is called, is the only one of the three being publicly exhibited.

Large acquisitions, such as the Besser collection, were followed by extensive cataloging. Friedrich August II, like his father a passionate collector, wanted rapid recataloging of the entire collection after he acquired the Besser library—a demand that temporarily stopped all lending. Card catalogs and manuscript and map inventories were all updated. In addition, all illustrations and maps of cities and fortresses available in print were cataloged. These improvements increased the use of the library, which was kept open several hours a day. In 1753 the library began keeping a patrons' ledger, although only distinguished names were entered into it.

The Seven Years' War (1756–63) once again interrupted the growth of the Court Library. After the court and government had taken refuge in Warsaw and elsewhere, the Prussians in 1760 took Dresden by bombardment, destroying large sections of the city. The librarian saved the precious book collections by storing them in the vaults of the fortress.

By 1765 there was still no sign of economic recovery. Nevertheless, the Court Library in that year purchased the collection of Count Heinrich von Bünau (1697–1762), which comprised 42,000 volumes and was one of the most important scholarly libraries in Germany. Bünau's passion for book collecting had been kindled by working on a history of the German empire. The last volumes were never completed because of the war and Bünau's premature death. His library was noteworthy for its systematic classification and cataloging system, to which Johann Joachim Winckelmann, founder of classical archaeology, had contributed. The logic of that system is said to have motivated Winckelmann to develop his famous systematization, or periodization, of antiquities, which was the hallmark of his later magnum opus. It is due to Bünau's historical interests that large numbers of pamphlets from the period of the Thirty Years' War and many funeral orations have been preserved as historical sources.

Four years later, the even more comprehensive 62,000-volume library of the late Saxon prime minister, Count Heinrich von Brühl (1700–63), was acquired for 50,000 talers (10,000 more than was paid for Bünau's). The costly purchase underscores the Court Library's stature as a cultural institution, because at that time the treasury was very short of funds. If one considers that the priceless and coveted painting collection confiscated from the same estate had been auctioned off to the Russian tsarina, the purchase of Brühl's library becomes even more significant. Even during a time of poverty, the economic advantages expected from promoting scholarship were judged sufficient to justify the high cost of this book collection.

The collections of the two counts, Bünau and Brühl, complemented each other nicely. While the scholarly Bünau had limited his acquisitions to expensive folios, incunabula, manuscripts, or other rare items in support of his research, Brühl focused his passion for collecting on the arts, attempting to acquire everything that was aesthetically pleasing, costly, and rare. His collection of old foreign-language novels and plays was said to be the most comprehensive in Europe.

Johann Michael Francke (1717–75), Bünau's librarian and a colleague of Winckelmann, accompanied the collection and became a staff member of the Court Library, where he continued his pioneering work in cataloging. He advocated keeping the Bünau library intact and separate from the Court Library. However, his advice went unheeded, and he was forced to integrate Bünau's into the collections of the Court Library.

By this time the collections had grown enormously in size, and emphasis was now placed on balancing content, especially in the area of early editions. In 1773 the Court Library acquired the 1460 Gutenberg edition of the *Catholicon.* Additional efforts resulted in transfers of rare items from Saxon private schools that had received fragmented collections from monastic libraries. Among these books were many fragile early editions, such as Fust and Schöffer's Mainz *Psalterium* (1457), twenty-six incunabula from Chemnitz, and another twenty-four from Schneeberg. Thus, the Court Library gradually became the state depository. In 1822 the chief librarian, Friedrich Adolf Ebert (1791–1834), wrote: "Since the time of Friedrich August I the Court Library has been a true state library for Saxony and, as such, has preserved many things for the Fatherland, about which Saxony would boast abroad."

It soon became evident that the number of acquisitions would soon cause the Court Library to outgrow the space within the Zwinger. The elaborate Japanese Palace, after extensive renovation, became its new home in 1786. The newly appointed chief librarian, Johann Christoph Adelung (1786–1806), renamed the institution the Electoral Public Library (Kurfürstliche Öffentliche Bibliothek), and when Saxony became a kingdom in 1806, it became the Royal Public Library. Adelung, a scholar and also an able administrator, further enhanced the collections by acquiring important Old German manuscripts, such as an illuminated copy of the *Sachsenspiegel* (a medieval legal code written by Eike von Repgow), and other unique materials, such as a collection of 3,500 university dissertations.

Such a collection of literary treasures appealed to intellectuals such as Johann Christoph Friedrich von Schiller, Johann Gottfried von Herder, and Heinrich von Kleist, all of whom made use of the library. Similarly, many European travelers visited the collections in the Japanese Palace, as did several rulers, such as Kaiser Leopold II of Austria, King Friedrich Wilhelm II of Prussia, and Napoleon.

The significant reduction of the Saxon territory decreed by the Congress of Vienna in 1815 weakened the kingdom both politically and economically, with serious consequences for the budget and development of the Royal Public Library. By 1834 it was evident that the Royal Public Library with its 300,000 volumes had been surpassed in size by the Bavarian Court Library, and in contemporary literature its collection was inferior to that of the University of Göttingen.

The Library Takes a New Direction

Although the Dresden library no longer surpassed other libraries in expanding its collections, it remained a leader in librarianship. Such Dresden chief librarians as Friedrich Adolf Ebert (1791–1834) and Ernst Förstemann (1865–87) gained national recognition by encouraging bibliography and librarianship. As early as 1816 the Royal Public Library had become a pioneer of modern library administration, when it established one of the first music departments in a German library, and by 1835 it installed cases for displaying library treasures to the public. A century later the space devoted to the display of library treasures had grown into a book museum of several rooms.

By the middle of the nineteenth century, as a result of the sharp increase in book production, the library was no longer able to collect universally, a practice that it had always promoted and defended. Librarian Petzholdt wrote in 1843 in the *Wegweiser für Dresdner Bibliotheken*—probably the first library guide in Germany—that one of the reasons for the gaps in the Royal Public Library was insufficient funds, but that the ultimate cause was the existence of specialized libraries, such as the Dresden Polytechnic Library. The Royal Library limited its acquisitions of scientific and technical literature—in spite of the high demand for such works—and stopped acquiring medical literature altogether, since the Dresden Medical Academy Library had taken over responsibility for collecting literature in this area.

With each library assuming responsibility for its subject specialty, Förstemann, during his tenure at the Royal Public Library, targeted the areas of history and its ancillary disciplines, geography, political science, belles lettres, and art and music. In history, geography, and local history, the systematic acquisition of materials relating to Saxony, or Saxonica, brought large numbers of Saxon chronicles, family records, and unpublished works into the library. Of special significance was the acquisition of a collection of 317 original prints from the period of the Reformation. In 1880 the Royal Public Library became one of the first libraries in Germany to specialize in the bibliography of regional studies.

As chief librarian, Franz Schnorr von Carolsfeld (1887–1907) focused on the printed music collection. Together with the Saxon Antiquarian Association, he perused the holdings of numerous Saxon churches and schools to obtain their printed music collections for the Royal Public Library. These complemented the royal private music collection of 4,000 volumes and 300 cases (holding thousands of items)—a singularly complete archive of eighteenth- and nineteenth-century court music. Together with the liturgical music, the manuscript material for more than a thousand operas composed for and/or performed at the Dresden court, in addition to autograph scores by Johann Sebastian Bach, Carl Maria von Weber, Richard Wagner, Antonio Vivaldi, and many other famous composers, formed a unique music archive that is still heavily used by the music industry, for example, in the Dresden Music Festival.

In the early twentieth century the growth of the library was disrupted by World War I (1914–18), inflation, and the world economic crisis. Book acquisitions declined dramatically, and for a time the library was cut off from its foreign suppliers.

After the Weimar Republic was proclaimed in 1919, the Royal Public Library and all the former court libraries were renamed the Saxon State Library, reflecting the true function of the institution as a central scholarly library for the state of Saxony.

Despite poor economic and political conditions, library director Martin Bollert (1920–37) continued to expand the Saxon State Library. He remodeled the Japanese Palace to increase use of the collections. A frugal administrator in lean times, Bollert made the Saxon State Library a model in Germany of the modern, efficient research and general library, at a time when many state libraries were undergoing an identity crisis. Until World War II, the Saxon State Library ranked third among German libraries in the scope and size of its special collections and continued to be a leader in the field of German librarianship.

The Nazi Period and Its Aftermath

National Socialist domination and World War II put an end to the progress the Saxon State Library had made under Bollert's direction. Bollert himself was not prepared to conform to the requirements of the Nazi regime and was sent into early retirement. The few Jewish staff members were forced to resign, and Jewish users of the library were forced to stay away because the Nuremberg Race Laws (1935) prohibited them from entering theaters, movies, or libraries.

Countless books were also victims of Hitler's barbarism, including those of Heinrich and Thomas Mann, Bertolt Brecht, and Sigmund Freud. Annual lists were published of prohibited or undesirable literature to be removed from the shelves. None of these titles was destroyed at the Saxon State Library, but the use of "undesirable" books was severely restricted. Libraries of exiled or expatriate Jewish citizens were considered undesirable acquisitions. They were not added to the collection but were kept separate from the other books—on "deposit," as it were—until they could be returned to their owners.

After the war began in 1939 the precious holdings of old books were moved to eighteen castles and offices in the vicinity of Dresden, where they survived the war safely. During the night of 13 February 1945, British Air Force squadrons razed the inner city. The Japanese Palace was hit hard but only partially destroyed. On 2 March American bombers completed the work of destruction. The results of both air raids included the death of four library employees while on the nightly fire watch, the loss of the magnificent Japanese Palace, and the destruction of about 200,000 volumes, primarily of twentieth-century literature. In addition there was damage to the most precious parts of the collection, which had been carefully stored in a vault considered proof against fire, water, and bombs. The violence of the bomb explosions cracked the thick walls of the vault, letting water in to do its destructive work on priceless manuscripts and old editions. Even today, the library's restoration workshop is dealing with the water damage to preserve these treasures from further disintegration.

After the war, the undamaged collections stored in the basement of the Japanese Palace, together with parts of the old collection that had been evacuated and then brought back, were housed in new provisional quarters on the north side of Dresden, where they have remained to this day.

The Saxon State Library suffered yet another loss when Soviet occupation troops confiscated 220,000 printed works dating from the fifteenth to the nineteenth century, as well as the manuscript and map collections, and took them to the Soviet Union. These special collections had remained in storage after evacuation due to lack of transportation to or space in the library.

Despite the obvious need for haste, the cultural official in charge of confiscation, who was also the director of the Moscow Foreign Literature Library, did not proceed haphazardly or indiscriminately. The boxes that were carried away contained those parts of the library collection that would best complement the holdings of Soviet libraries, which had been severely damaged in the war. Consequently, the Russians chose not to take the Saxonica and Slavic collections of the Saxon State Library.

In an intergovernmental agreement, the Soviet Union and the German Democratic Republic (GDR) in 1958 repatriated the manuscript collection and the paintings of the Dresden Gallery of Art. The printed book collections, however, remained in the Soviet Union, and their location was concealed until the 1980s. The GDR halted attempts to uncover the whereabouts of these treasures. Only after the events of 1989 in central and eastern Europe was an agreement reached for the mutual return of all cultural assets. In 1993 materials of the Saxon State Library were identified in three large Moscow libraries, but none of these items has yet been returned.

The Library Asserts Itself

In 1952 the government of the GDR dissolved the individual states and eliminated the political mandate for state libraries. Only the Saxon State Library was able to retain its status, to assert its traditions, and to secure new functions within the GDR library system.

The first tasks facing the Saxon State Library were to eliminate all fascist and militaristic literature from its holdings and to try to rebuild lost collections. Holdings of abandoned or little used libraries throughout the GDR were consolidated and added to the Dresden collections. The libraries of Saxon teachers' colleges, gymnasia, societies and associations, and castles, nationalized in the 1946 land reform act, brought a wealth of material to the Saxon State Library. Although funding was limited, the Saxon State Library also acquired new publications, both foreign and domestic.

Although the "Western literature" section had special importance, the library could make it available only to special readers, that is, subject specialists. The removal of Western periodicals from the reading room was mandated in 1980.

For the Saxon State Library to meet its goal of providing broad scholarly literature, it had to acquire West German, American, and British books and periodicals, not only East German and Soviet literature. However, little hard currency was available to purchase Western publications. The Saxon State Library, therefore, developed an active international exchange program that allowed it to acquire a significant amount of literature from the West. Several exchanges took place between the Saxon State Library and the Library of Congress, forming the basis for the present-day cooperation between the two institutions. For example, the Saxon State Library provided the Library of Congress with its *Saxon Bibliography* (begun in 1961), the *GDR Bibliography of Art* (1973–88), and the *Music Bibliography* (1974–89). The library's bibliographical work focused on its specialization in art, music, and general and local history. This effort resulted in the library's designation in the 1980s as the Central Library for Art and Music in the GDR.

Library director Burghard Burgemeister (1959–90) was largely responsible for these accomplishments. He was able to protect the Saxon State Library against the intervention of state bureaucrats and simultaneously expand the special collections. He further transformed the institution into one of the most important media centers in the German library system by merging the Deutsche Fototek and its 1.8 million pictorial documents into the library, establishing a Recorded Sound Division numbering 150,000 items, and integrating into the holdings the world's largest collection of stenographic manuscripts and books.

When the Free State of Saxony was reestablished in 1990 as part of German unification, the Saxon State Library once again became the state library of Saxony.

It had always been the central academic library and the archive for regional culture in Saxony.

Nineteen ninety-six is the four hundred fortieth anniversary of the founding of the Saxon State Library. The library has now been merged with the library of Dresden Technical University, which has become a comprehensive university with the addition of literature and information sciences to its curriculum. Combining the two libraries affords an opportunity to establish an even more dynamic library of international stature.

Detail, Illustration 11

Reinhardt Eigenwill

Political Ambition versus Cultural Commitment: The House of Wettin

German history is often viewed from a Prussian perspective or—at least for the period before the end of the German Confederation in 1866—an Austrian perspective. Although most of the smaller German states eventually lost their political autonomy to the powerful state of Prussia, they nevertheless played a major role in Germany's thousand-year history. Among these Saxony stands out. From the Middle Ages on it was for centuries an important territory, both politically and economically. It also is to this day one of the leading cultural centers of Germany.

The Origins of the House of Wettin

The House of Wettin dates back to the tenth century. Its members were first margraves, then dukes, later electors and kings. The Wettins, one of the oldest German families, left their mark on the history of Saxony and also on that of central Germany, at times playing a significant role in the history of the empire. Margrave Konrad the Great (d. 1157) solidly established Wettin rule in Meissen and the surrounding area during a period when political and social conditions allowed the power of the princes to become greater than the central power of the king. Konrad's position was so secure that before his death he bequeathed his territory to his sons without the consent of the emperor, Frederick Barbarossa.

Konrad's oldest son Otto (d. 1190) inherited the Meissen margravate and took advantage of the opportunities offered by the great economic, social, and political upheavals of the High Middle Ages. During the period of German colonization eastward, he had large forested areas cleared to build settlements and was also instrumental in founding the first cities within his margravate: Leipzig (founded 1160) and Freiberg (1168). These new cities served as centers of trade and commerce, and also of political support. The discovery of silver deposits in the eastern part of the Erzgebirge (Ore Mountains) laid the foundation for Saxony's economic power and for the ruler's designation as Otto the Rich.

In 1162 Otto founded the Altzelle Monastery as the private sanctuary of the Wettin margraves, and it long remained the cultural center of the margravate of Meissen. Here, as in other European monasteries, members of religious orders produced by hand unsurpassed illuminated manuscripts.

In spite of the rise of the House of Wettin under Konrad the Great and Otto the Rich, the balance of power between the king and the imperial princes remained fragile and the princes' position far from consolidated. At the end of the twelfth century the powerful Hohenstaufen emperor Henry VI confiscated the margravate of Meissen, threatening the existence of the House of Wettin. Only the emperor's sudden death enabled Margrave Dietrich (d. 1221) to win back Meissen for the Wettins. Dietrich survived the turmoil surrounding the dispute over the throne between the Staufen and Welf dynasties, and even strengthened his rule through the founding of new cities, such as Dresden.

In 1247 the power of the House of Wettin reached new heights under Margrave Heinrich the Exalted (d. 1288), whose inheritance claims and excellent relations with the imperial House of Hohenstaufen brought him the landgravate of Thüringen. A few years earlier, the Pleissenland region around Altenburg had come into the possession of the margravate as the dowry of Margarethe, daughter of Emperor Frederick II and the betrothed of Heinrich's son Albrecht. Heinrich also expanded his position in the east with the founding of the city of Fürstenberg and the monastery of Neuzelle. He was famous among his contemporaries for the splendor of his court. His residences were centers of the chivalric and courtly culture of the time. The margrave himself even composed religious songs.

The Rise of the Wettins

The possessor of land stretching from the Werra River in the west to the Oder River in the east, Heinrich the Illustrious was one of the most important princes of the empire, yet he was unable to expand the power of the House of Wettin. Heinrich's grandson, Friedrich the Bold—son of Margarethe and grandson of the last Hohenstaufen emperor—even made a futile claim to the imperial crown. The attempt failed in part because of massive resistance by the papacy to any effort to restore Hohenstaufen rule and in part because of quarrels within the Wettin family. The Wettins, the longest reigning dynasty in German history, attempted such power grabs only rarely, but in all cases these efforts failed.

The period following Heinrich's reign saw additional upheaval within the House of Wettin and struggles against the renewed strength of the king. At this time the situation appeared more threatening for the House of Wettin than it had during the reign of Emperor Henry VI. At times the Meissen margravate came directly under the rule of the king. Friedrich the Bold (d. 1323) reestablished the former power of the House of Wettin. In a battle fought near Lucka in 1307, the Wettin troops decisively defeated the forces of King Albrecht of Habsburg.

During the fourteenth century the margraves asserted themselves against the power politics of Emperor Charles IV. The early fifteenth century brought a surprising and decisive upswing in the fortunes of the House of Wettin. In 1423, after the last of the Ascanian dukes of Saxe-Wittenberg had died, Emperor Sigismund bequeathed the duchy of Saxony to Friedrich the Warlike (d. 1428) for his assistance in the emperor's fight against the Hussites, religious reformers who were followers of John Hus. The duchy carried with it electoral status.

This gift represented a major advance in the stature of the margrave, who thereby became one of the seven imperial princes who had the right to elect the German king. This development laid the foundation both for the politically significant role that the Albertine line of the Wettin dynasty played from the sixteenth to the eighteenth century and for the cultural and economic development of the Saxon states from the outset of the sixteenth century. From the end of the fifteenth century, the name Saxony was gradually applied also to the Meissen margravate and other possessions of the House of Wettin. Friedrich, the first Wettin Saxon elector, was buried in the funeral chapel of Meissen Cathedral, which he founded.

In 1409 Friedrich and his brother Wilhelm had founded the University of Leipzig, following a dispute between the German students and the University of Prague, which had denied them the right to vote for a president. The students took advantage of the situation to open a new university in Leipzig, which received the official sanction of the Wettins.

Land Partition: Setbacks and Growth

In 1482, during the joint rule of the brothers Ernst and Albrecht the Brave, which had begun in 1464, the estates of the Wettin dynasty were united. At that time other members of the family were archbishops of Mainz and Magdeburg. Never before had the House of Wettin attained such a position of power. But three years after union, Elector Ernst (d. 1486) initiated the unfortunate partition of the Wettin lands. Elector Ernst received, in addition to his electoral area of Wittenberg, the greater part of the Thüringian possessions of the House of Wettin and parts of the margravate of Meissen. Albrecht received the larger part of the margravate of Meissen and a few parts of the Thüringian possessions of the Wettins. This decision ran contrary to the growing tendency to centralize economic and political power. Although the land partition was not intended to be permanent, nonetheless the Ernestine and Albertine lines went their separate ways from that time on. The chance for future Wettin dominance in the eastern part of Germany had passed. Duke Albrecht (d. 1500) prevented further division of Albertine Saxony by passing the law of primogeniture in 1499.

Despite the unfavorable land partition of 1485, the Wettin territories in the sixteenth century were among the most progressive areas of Germany. Their great economic resources were based on the east–west trade of the famous Leipzig fair and the renewed mining in the Erzgebirge at the end of the fifteenth century. At the same time, the cultural and intellectual forces of humanism, the Renaissance, and the Reformation resulted in unexpected economic, political, and cultural energy. Under the dynamic leadership of the Albertines—Duke Albrecht the Brave and his successors Georg, Moritz, and August—this energy found practical application.

Duke Albrecht commissioned the construction of the Gothic Castle in Meissen, considered the first uniquely German castle. Duke Georg (d. 1539) concerned himself with improving finances and administering his lands, despite the political and religious troubles of the time. In addition, he began the construction and expansion of Dresden, the capital city of Albertine Saxony. He was a powerful opponent of the religious views of Martin Luther, but his struggle to have the Albertine duchy of Saxony retain allegiance to the Roman Catholic Church met with failure. He was succeeded by his brother Heinrich the Pious (d. 1541), who had already converted to the Lutheran faith. With the support of Elector Johann Friedrich the Magnanimous (d. 1547), of the Ernestine line, Heinrich officially introduced the Reformation into Albertine Saxony in July 1539.

Duke Moritz (d. 1553), son and successor of Heinrich, was perhaps the most politically astute member of the House of Wettin. He very soon learned to understand and anticipate the diplomatic chess moves of Emperor Charles V, and he decisively led Albertine Saxony to the forefront of the Protestant states. At the same time, he made it the most powerful territory of the empire, except for the areas ruled by the Habsburgs. In the city of Schmalkalden in 1531, several important German princes and cities had formed an alliance to defend Protestant interests against Emperor Charles V. As a result of the Schmalkaldic War of 1547, Duke Moritz was able to wrest more territory from his Ernestine relations, along with the actual duchy of

Saxony with its electoral status. Even he, however, could not completely compensate for the 1485 territorial partition. With the 1552 Treaty of Passau he secured the "liberty" of the imperial princes and the continuation of Protestantism.

Art and Politics in the Sixteenth Century

Elector Moritz, although less interested in the arts and sciences than his predecessors had been, made significant cultural contributions to enhance his political position. These included additions to the Dresden Castle, construction of the Moritzburg hunting castle near Dresden, and the expansion of Leipzig University. He also founded three *Fürstenschulen* (princely schools) in 1543 in Meissen, Grimma, and Pforta, and in 1548 he established the Court Orchestra, the forerunner of the Dresden State Orchestra. The early death at age thirty-two of this outstanding Renaissance ruler has led historians to speculate whether, had he lived, both Saxon and German history might have taken a different course.

Moritz was succeeded by his brother August (d. 1586), who did not pursue a bold foreign policy. Intending to maintain a balance to the emperor, he effectively renounced an active leadership role among the Protestant states and instead focused his efforts on the internal development of electoral Saxony. Among his accomplishments were stimulation of the economy, improved organization of the administrative and judicial systems, better church organization, and strong support for the arts and sciences. Saxony enjoyed unprecedented prosperity over other German territories—an advantage that it was able to maintain, at least in part, into the first half of the twentieth century. Among August's many cultural contributions was the creation of the Dresden Court Library (today the Saxon State Library), based on his private library. In 1560 he founded an art gallery. Having a strong interest in architecture, as well as many other aspects of the arts, he invited Italian artists to his court. The Dresden armory and the Augustusburg and Annaburg castles were tributes to his initiative. In the Freiberg princes' mausoleum, he built an impressive tomb to honor his predecessor. Historical accounts of the Albertine Wettin dynasty document the commitment of these rulers to the enhancement of the political, social, and cultural life of their subjects.

The Political Prospects of Saxony

Under Elector Christian I (d. 1591) and his chancellor Nikolaus Krell, electoral Saxony once again assumed an active political role in the empire and beyond. Although Krell sought to break the power of the nobility in Saxony and to introduce Calvinism, the early death of Christian I ended these plans. In foreign politics, Saxony found itself again within the Austrian Habsburg sphere. From the victory of the nobility and Lutheran orthodoxy arose the typical patriarchal and conservative features of the administration of Saxony.

During the devastating Thirty Years' War, the Albertine line of the House of Wettin overestimated its influence on the course of political events, changing allegiance from the emperor to the Swedes and back again. Despite suffering heavy war losses, Saxony was able to recover rapidly because of its economic resources. The long-term political prospects of Saxony had declined under Johann Georg I (d. 1656), even though, as a result of this war, he had won both parts of the Lausitz region in 1635. With the transfer of the territory of the secularized former archbishopric from Magdeburg to Brandenburg, the political importance of the dynasty of the Albertine Wettins was further reduced. In his will of 1652 Johann Georg I further weakened Saxony's position by creating three separate Albertine lines out of his electoral Saxon dynasty while upholding the supremacy of the electoral line. The three lines of the dukes of Saxony-Merseburg, Saxony-Weissenfels, and Saxony-Zeitz died out in the first half of the eighteenth century, and their possessions were reintegrated into electoral Saxony.

The Baroque Period in Saxony

The baroque period began in Saxony with the reign of Johann Georg II (d. 1680), who loved splendor and ostentation. Art and culture flourished at his court. After 1664 the architect Wolf Caspar von Klengel built the first opera house in Dresden, and in 1676 the great garden near the princely residence was laid out. In 1678 Johann Georg II, with the rulers of the three collateral Albertine lines, held an "Assembly of Their Highnesses" in Dresden. It was a precursor of the great baroque court festivals of the eighteenth century. A dynamic economy was largely responsible for providing the funds needed for these expensive cultural projects.

Music and theater played a prominent role in the life of the court. Italian opera dominated music, and French plays captured the theater. Johann Georg III (d. 1691) was the first German prince to have Molière's plays performed at court. The performances were preceded by contests and court festivals in the princely residence and at other locations in Saxony.

In the late 1600s the foreign policy of the Albertine lines, in accordance with the traditional loyalty to the empire, was also oriented toward the House of Habsburg. The Albertine Wettins supported the Habsburgs in the struggle against the Turks and against the expansionist policy of Louis XIV of France. However, Johann Georg II was also at times closely allied to France, receiving large subsidies for his support from the French government.

With the reign of Elector Friedrich August I (August the Strong, d. 1733) began the so-called "Augustan period," which lasted until the Seven Years' War (1756–63). Under his rule the Dresden court was known as one of the most splendid in Germany and in all of Europe. Many important artists were drawn to Dresden. Architecture, music, and the other arts and crafts all flourished under August the Strong and his successor Friedrich August II (d. 1763). Many architectural masterpieces were constructed in Dresden and its environs: the Zwinger, Pillnitz Castle, the Frauenkirche, and the Catholic Court Church. Other architectural gems, including many palaces of the nobility, were built by such prominent architects as Matthäus Daniel Pöppelmann, Georg Bähr, Gaetano Chiaveri, and Johann Christoph Knöffel. The palaces and churches were decorated by sculptors such as Balthasar Permoser and Lorenzo Matielli.

In 1721 Elector Friedrich August I founded the art gallery's Grünes Gewölbe (Green Vault) and had it embellished with the works of the famous goldsmith Melchior Dinglinger. In 1754 he and his successor acquired the Raphael *Sistine Madonna* for the Dresden Royal Gallery. As well as a passionate collector of paintings, Friedrich August II was also, along with his wife Princess Maria Josephine of Habsburg, very interested in music. This era, when the Court Orchestra was directed by conductor Johann Adolph Hasse, is well known to musicologists.

The Decline of Saxon Power

The cultural accomplishments of the Augustan period would not have been possible without the economic strength of the state, clearly demonstrated by the growing importance of the Leipzig trade fairs. Leipzig was the most important center for trade between central and eastern Europe, in particular for the exchange of Saxon industrial products and eastern European raw materials, such as furs. Together with his strong aesthetic sense, August the Strong combined political ambition and a remarkable vitality that permitted him to follow his ambitious plans in two directions over the course of his long reign. His domestic policy was aimed at crushing the power of the nobility, while his foreign policy envisioned the establishment of an east-central European empire that could claim its rightful place among the great powers of Europe. His ascent to the Polish throne in 1697, as King August II, was seen as a first step in this direction. However, because of his conversion to Catholicism, Saxony lost its leading position among the Protestant states to Brandenburg-Prussia. August the Strong's ambitions included gaining additional territories of the House of Habsburg (whose male line was expected to die out at the beginning of the eighteenth century) and ultimately acquiring the imperial crown for the House of Wettin.

For all his support of the arts, as collector, patron, and even the contributor of ideas to different projects, August the Strong never lost sight of his political goals. More than almost any other German baroque prince, he was aware of his standing as a ruler. The extravagant court festivals he sponsored also served his political ambitions. For example, the famous court festival near the town of Zeithain in 1730 combined baroque pomp and pageantry with the display of military and political might.

The reign of this unusual member of the House of Wettin presents a contradictory picture. In foreign policy, he overestimated his power and what could be attained by the Albertine branch, especially in competition with the aspiring state of Brandenburg-Prussia. Although gifted in many ways, he lacked the tenacity to concentrate on long-range goals. Yet even though August the Strong was largely unable to realize his ambitious political goals, his strong influence on the cultural history of Saxony remains undisputed.

For his successor, Friedrich August II, an opera performance was always more important than the burdensome daily routine of affairs of state, as Frederick the Great noted scornfully in his memoirs. Friedrich August II was dominated by his powerful minister Count Heinrich von Brühl, and during the War of the Austrian Succession (1740–58) he lost the political prestige of Saxony that had been won by his father.

During the Seven Years' War the situation worsened as Saxony became a pawn of the powers involved. It quickly recovered from the economic aftermath of the war, however, as economic and political reforms were enacted. With the gradual establishment of bourgeois society, the role of the monarch was weakened even further. Upon the death of August II in 1763 the Polish-Saxon personal union was dissolved, and gradually Saxony exerted less and less influence on the course of German history. Like the other smaller German states, it was increasingly subject to the hegemony of Prussia and Austria.

During the Napoleonic wars the "Holy Roman Empire of the German Nation" collapsed. In the battles of October 1806 near Jena and Auerstädt, the Saxon elector's troops initially fought with the Prussians, who were defeated. Subsequently, the Albertine branch, assuming royal status, switched allegiance and became loyal supporters of Napoleon. At the Congress of Vienna in 1815 Saxony was on the losing side and was forced to surrender more than half its territory to Prussia.

Although its political influence continued to decline, the Saxon royal house liked to believe that its cultural patronage somewhat balanced these losses. However, the first constitution and the ensuing civil reforms of 1831–32 separated the state and court budgets, further limiting the ruler's activities. The museums and other cultural institutions, while still legally in the possession of the royal house, were now subject to state control and were administered according to the constitution.

The reign of King Friedrich August II (d. 1854) coincided with the era preceding the bourgeois-democratic revolution that culminated in the 1849 uprising at Dresden. The revolution was crushed, delaying the collapse of the old authoritarian monarchical system. Still, over this period a modern bourgeois society gradually prevailed.

In the era of the industrial revolution, which began in Germany in Saxony and the Rhineland, the monarchy and nobility had less opportunity for their own development. King Friedrich August II established the collection of copper engravings in Dresden and commissioned buildings by Gottfried Semper. King Johann of Saxony (d. 1873), a renowned scholar, produced among other things a German translation of Dante's *Divine Comedy* that is still used today. This latter endeavor reflects the private, almost intimate quality of Wettin cultural activity in the 1860s.

Saxony, initially aligned with the Austrian monarchy during the Austro-Prussian War of 1866, became a member of the Prussian-led North German Confederation. At the end of the Franco-Prussian War in 1871 it became a state within the German Empire founded by Bismarck. The November Revolution of 1918, following World War I, brought an end to the monarchy in Saxony. King Friedrich August III (d. 1932) abdicated on 13 November 1918, exclaiming, "Do your own dirty work!" (Macht Euren Dreck alleene).

As an independent state and one of the most economically well-developed areas of Germany, Saxony played an important part in the history of the Weimar Republic, especially in the political and social struggles of that time. It survived the devastation of World War II and became part of the Soviet Occupation Zone after 1945 and, after 1949, part of the German Democratic Republic. However, the events of 1989 and the unification of Germany in 1990 made Saxony a free state once again.

The House of Wettin

Friedrich II the Gentle	1428–64	Elector	
Ernst	1464–86	Elector	*His descendants formed the Ernestinian line.*
Albrecht the Brave	1464–85	Coregent	*His descendants formed the Albertine line.*
Friedrich the Wise	1486–1525	Elector	
Johann the Constant	1525–32	Elector	
Georg the Bearded	1500–39	Duke	
Heinrich the Pious	1539–41	Duke	
Johann Friedrich the Magnanimous	1532–47	Elector	
Moritz	1541–47	Duke	
	1547–53	Elector	
August	1553–86	Elector	
Christian I	1586–91	Elector	
Christian II	1591–1611	Elector	
Johann Georg I	1611–56	Elector	
Johann Georg II	1656–80	Elector	
Johann Georg III	1680–91	Elector	
Johann Georg IV	1691–94	Elector	
Friedrich August I	1694–1733	Elector	*Became king of Poland in 1697.*
Friedrich August II	1733–63	Elector	
Friedrich Christian	1763	Elector	
Friedrich August III (I)	1763–1806	Elector	
	1806–27	King	
Anton			
Maximilian	1827–36	King	
Friedrich August II	1836–54	King	
Johann	1854–73	King	
Albert	1873–1902	King	
Johann	1902–04	King	
Friedrich August III	1904–18	King	

Prepared by Eberhard Stimmel

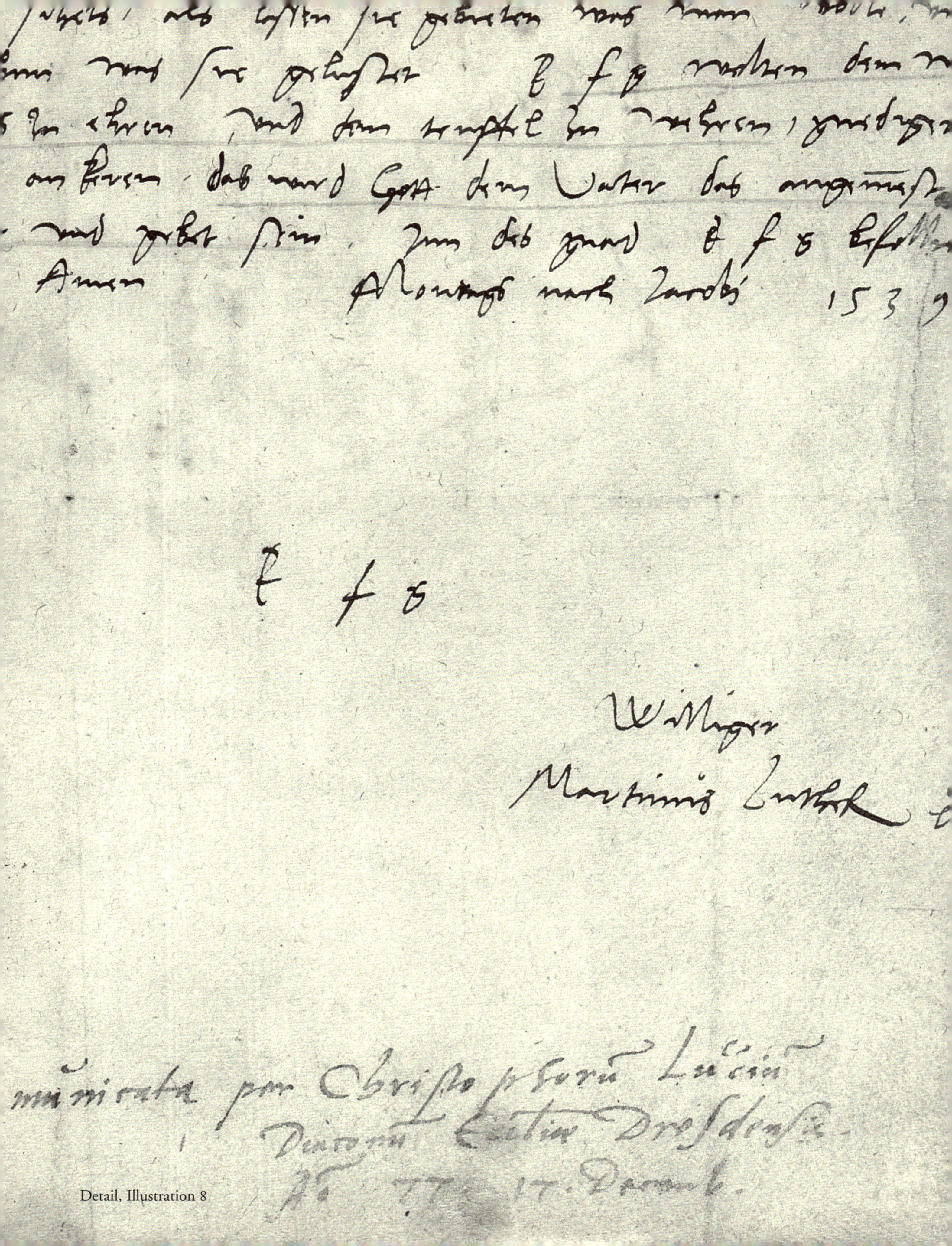

Detail, Illustration 8

Christian Zühlke

The Protestant Reformation in Saxony

The Protestant Reformation began in Saxony and constitutes one of Saxony's most significant contributions to world history. Arising from the Reformation were the Lutheran, Reformed, and Anglican churches, as well as other religious movements, such as the Puritans and Quakers, all of which profoundly influenced the political, economic, and cultural life of Europe and North America.

The German Reformation is primarily associated with Martin Luther (1483–1546). Luther's opposition to the Catholic Church's practice of selling indulgences developed into a powerful mass movement. Fearing divine punishment, the faithful purchased indulgences to ensure their absolution for past and future sins. The Catholic Church used the proceeds to finance the sumptuous lifestyle of the pope and archbishops, as well as to subsidize construction of new churches, monasteries, and abbeys. Luther's opposition to indulgences might have remained simply a part of theological history if not for the more general social, economic, and political problems of the time, which had developed into a dangerous powder keg waiting to be ignited.

Luther was not the first theologian to express reformist ideas. However, he gave new life to such views and thus became the principal force behind the

Reformation, a religious and social movement whose criticism of spiritual decay in the Roman Catholic Church and the papacy was rooted in the High Middle Ages.

On 31 October 1517 Luther, an Augustinian monk and professor of biblical studies at the Saxon University of Wittenberg, sent to his church superiors letters written in Latin in which he enclosed "95 Theses on the Power of Indulgences." He intended to challenge others to a theological debate, or scholarly disputation—a commonplace activity among scholars at that time. Luther also sent the theses to his friends in Nuremberg. The legend that Luther personally nailed the theses to the door of Wittenberg Castle Church is based on an account written in 1546 by Philipp Melanchthon (1497–1560), who was not even present in Wittenberg in 1517.

The immediate motivation behind the "95 Theses" was the appearance in Saxony of one of the most persistent sellers of indulgences, the Dominican friar Johann Tetzel (c. 1465–1519), who had a large following, even in Saxony where the trade in indulgences was unlawful. Pope Julius II (1503–13) had just issued an indulgence for the construction of St. Peter's Church in Rome. The papal commissioner of indulgences in Germany was one of Luther's superiors, Archbishop Albrecht of Mainz (1490–1545), who was deeply in debt as a result of the 29,000 gulden he had sent to Rome to obtain various positions. The Fugger banking house in Augsburg had advanced him the money in the belief that his position as commissioner of indulgences would enable him to settle his debts. (The commissioner was allowed to keep half the amount acquired from the sale of indulgences.) Tetzel, who was always accompanied by an official of the Fuggers, sought to increase his proceeds with sayings like this: "As soon as the money falls into the box, souls will jump from the fires of Hell into Heaven." Claims such as this were too much for Luther to accept.

Luther's view of indulgences grew out of his so-called "tower experience": the basic theological concepts of God's justice he had acquired while working, in his study in the Wittenberg monastery tower, on an exegesis of the biblical passage Romans 1:17. Luther believed that all efforts to earn God's grace through good works (indulgences, fasting, pilgrimages, entry into a monastery, the financing of masses, and so forth) are of no value. God does not require righteousness but rather grants it in faith: He is a merciful God, not a punishing God. Salvation (Luther's question: "How do I obtain God's grace?") is attainable only through faith *(sola fide)*. The person who believes, "be he a sinner or a righteous man," is forgiven through grace and not because he has somehow "earned" salvation. In this view, the buying and selling of indulgences made the forgiveness of sin "a holy commodity" to be obtained with money.

Luther's new theological statement was developed step by step between 1513 and 1518 as preparation for his lectures on the Psalms and on Saint Paul's letters to the Romans, Galatians, and Hebrews. It was the real message of the Reformation. When he sent out his theses, however, Luther did not foresee any reformation of the Church. He intended only to oppose the abusive practice of the sale of indulgences by subordinate church offices.

In 1517 the "95 Theses" were printed in Latin in a one-page format in Leipzig and Nuremberg, and a short time later they were printed in Basel in book form. German translations quickly followed. Duke Georg of Saxony (Georg the Bearded, d. 1539) allowed them to be circulated to warn of Tetzel's deception and to stop the illegal trade in indulgences.

A literary war of unprecedented dimensions followed. Luther's simple, colloquial writing style appealed to the people. The printing and book trade gave Luther access to the reading public and an unexpectedly wide audience and influence. In the next two years 38 manuscripts by Luther were printed in 113 editions in Leipzig alone—40 percent of all his writings printed before 1519—an indication of the city's importance in the publishing trade. After 1520 Wittenberg became the preferred place of publication for reformist writings. The pope tried to silence Luther through his superiors, but their attempts failed, and charges of heresy were levied against him. Luther's sovereign, Elector Friedrich the Wise (d. 1525), managed to arrange for Luther to answer the charges before the papal legate Cardinal Cajetan (Thomas de Vio from Gaeta, 1469–1534) at the next imperial Diet in Augsburg, rather than in Rome. The hearing in October 1518 produced no result, nor did a conversation in January 1519 with the papal diplomat Karl von Miltitz (1490–1529) from

Dresden. Luther pointed out that he could not be forced to recant if he had not committed an error.

A debate in Leipzig from 27 June to 16 July 1519 was more productive and enabled Luther to advance his theological concepts. It also brought him new followers, as well as opponents, and divided the two Saxon states along denominational lines. Duke Georg was Luther's nemesis, but out of a desire to shock his theologians "out of their peace and idleness," he ordered the Theological Faculty in Leipzig to open its premises to the debate. The event took place at the Pleissenburg, because the university auditorium could not accommodate everyone who wished to attend. During the first week Andreas Bodenstein, called Karlstadt (1486–1541), and Johann Eck (1486–1543) argued on the topic of free will. In the second week, Luther and Eck debated the question of the authority of the pope and the Church councils. Pressed by Eck, Luther rejected the concept of the pope's primacy and his indispensability for granting salvation; this was not God's but man's will. Moreover, he held that the pope and the councils could err, and that the Council of Constance had condemned statements by Jan Hus that were Christian and based on the Gospels. With this, Eck had what he needed: Luther was shown to be a "Saxon Hus" and a heretic. Duke Georg was painfully aware that he himself was the grandson of the "Hussite heretic king" Georg von Podiebrad (1420–71).

Whether intentionally or by accident, the argument over indulgences developed into a dispute over the foundations of the Roman Catholic Church. This in turn won Luther additional followers, above all from the circle of humanists, including his most important ally, Philipp Melanchthon. Other south German supporters of Luther included Ulrich von Hutten (1488–1523) and Willibald Pirckheimer (1470–1530), as well as Pirckheimer's friend, the painter Albrecht Dürer (1471–1528). They supported Luther in letters and pamphlets. The Saxon State Library in Dresden has a collection of these Reformation pamphlets.

Luther was an extremely prolific writer. In his words, "a rapid hand and perfect memory" were his assets. In 1520, in addition to other texts, he published the three principal Reformation theses: *The Address to the Christian Nobility of the German Nation, The Babylonian Captivity of the Church,* and *The Freedom of the Christian Man.* These works were the foundation of the Reformation and carried the message of the movement into the country. The first 4,000 copies of the *Address to the Christian Nobility* sold out in a few days.

While Luther was writing his major theses, further measures were planned against him in Rome. With Eck's cooperation, a papal bull, warning of excommunication, was issued in June 1520, but Eck encountered difficulties in distributing the document in Germany. Nor was Friedrich the Wise prepared to permit distribution of the publication. By December 1520 Luther burned the papal bull before the Elster Gate in Wittenberg. Rome responded to this challenge by excommunicating Luther in January 1521.

According to law, excommunication from the Catholic Church was to be followed by a similar imperial ban. Elector Friedrich won agreement from the newly elected emperor Charles V that Luther should not be condemned without a hearing. In April 1521 Luther had to appear in Worms before the Diet, consisting of the emperor, the electors, and representatives of other states. In the Edict of Worms (May 1521) the Diet declared an imperial ban on Luther and his followers, ordered their writings to be burned, and placed all books appearing in Germany under church censorship. To protect him, Friedrich the Wise hid Luther in Wartburg Castle near Eisenach.

It is still unclear why Friedrich the Wise, who did not endorse the Reformation and who saw Luther only at the Diet of Worms, protected him, thus encouraging the spread of the Reformation. It may be that Friedrich was motivated by a strong sense of justice. Perhaps the prestige of Wittenberg University, which he had founded in 1502, also played a role. When Luther taught there, enrollment increased (students even came from neighboring countries), while enrollment at its rival university in Leipzig declined. The pope tolerated Friedrich's attitude in view of the upcoming election of a new emperor.

While in hiding, Luther translated the New Testament into German, based on the Greek edition that Erasmus of Rotterdam (1466/69–1536) had published and translated into Latin. Luther completed the work in eleven weeks, and it appeared with a preface in September 1522 (the September Testament) in Wittenberg without naming either the translator or the printer. It was so successful that another edition was issued in December (the December Testament). Translation of the Old Testament followed in installments. By the time the first complete German-language Bible was published in 1534, the New Testament had reached a record printing: eighty-seven High German editions, nineteen Low German editions, three translations in Dutch, one in Danish, and one in Swedish. Luther's translation of the Bible set unprecedented standards for accuracy, greatly influencing the development of the new High German language. It also set standards for translating the Bible into different national languages, especially in states that endorsed the Reformation.

After Luther's Wartburg period, the Reformation developed its own momentum. In Wittenberg, which became the center of the movement, and in other cities, his followers began to apply his teachings to church life. Following the impressive Leipzig debate, individual Saxon priests had begun to preach *evangelisch* (according to the Gospels) in Leipzig, Döbeln, Grimma, the Lausitz area, Zittau, Görlitz, and Bautzen. Everywhere monks and nuns began to leave the monasteries, and priests took marriage vows long before Luther himself laid aside his monk's robe (16 October 1524) and married (13 June 1525). In January 1522 the German Augustinian congregation was dissolved in Wittenberg. In 1524 Duke Georg had to close the Celestine monastery on the Königstein when only the proctor remained. The situation was similar for the monasteries of other church orders. Many monks became pastors and devoted themselves to proclaiming the Reformation. In many cities councilmen urged the appointment of a Reform pastor, while others asked Luther to name a suitable candidate.

In Wittenberg Karlstadt, Justus Jonas (1493–1555), and Gabriel Zwilling (d. 1558) actively opposed indulgences and masses for the dead, and Karlstadt preached in secular dress on Christmas Day 1521 and administered the Lord's supper with bread and wine. These were revolutionary actions. In December, in the midst of this iconoclasm, the "Zwickau Prophets" arrived, with whom Thomas Müntzer (1489?–1525) was closely associated. Given their name by Luther, the "Zwickau Prophets" included the clothmakers Nikolaus Stovel and Thomas Drechsel, and former Wittenberg student Markus Thomas. Strongly pro-Reformation, they were also dreamers.

Luther was summoned and returned to Wittenberg on 6 March 1522. With his famous sermon on Invocavit Sunday, he tried to stop the iconoclastic excesses. He preached cautious reforms following sufficient spiritual preparation and protection of the weak. Everything associated with the idea of sacrifice was stricken from the mass, the confession, and also the private masses. In 1523 Luther's *Baptismal Booklet,* which made it possible for the sacrament of baptism to be conducted in the German language, appeared. This was followed in 1526 by his *German Mass and Order of Worship,* and in 1529 by the *Booklet on the Marriage Ceremony.*

With the elimination of priests to perform the mass, the new order set free all those funds that had been donated to subsidize worship services. The "Leisnig Collection Box Ruling" of 1523 (Leisnig is located between Leipzig and Dresden) was an example for other evangelical church organizations. This income for the parish and the church would go into a common collection box, which supported the pastor, sexton, schoolmaster, the poor, and orphans. Luther's *Ruling on the Common Collection Box* pointed out that the collection boxes should not be used to support beggar monks or pilgrims, as was sanctioned by church rules. His rules laid the foundation for the evangelical charitable organizations of today.

The Reformation was not a united movement. Through Huldrych Zwingli (1484–1531) and John Calvin (1509–64), it soon developed other centers and diversified. At the beginning of the Reformation, the "Zwickau Prophets" acquired a certain significance for Saxony, as did the German Peasants' War (1524–25). Although Luther's opponents liked to portray the situation differently, the peasant revolts were part of the social struggles of the late Middle Ages, which the Reformation accelerated but did not cause.

In regard to Karlstadt, it is unclear whether he was already a fanatic and iconoclast in his Wittenberg period or whether he became more consistent once reforms were introduced. Valentin Weigel (1533–88) belonged to the next generation of reformers. While conscientiously carrying out his pastoral duties in the small Saxon town of

Zschopau, he wrote works that he concealed in his desk or entrusted to a few friends. His writings, along with the ideas of the German mystic and natural philosopher Paracelsus (Theophrastus Bombastus von Hohenheim, 1493/94–1541), stand in a direct line from the radical wing of the Reformation to Jakob Böhme (1575–1624). Weigel's manuscripts, published after his death, created a great sensation in the seventeenth century.

After 1524 Germany began to divide into two denominational camps, and within Saxony there was a strict separation for the next fifteen years. Duke Georg continued to persecute every reformist movement or action in Albertine Saxony and ordered the expulsion of those of evangelical persuasion in a mandate of 1532, implemented especially in Leipzig. He encouraged his court chaplains, Hieronymus Emser (1477–1527) and Johannes Cochlaeus (1479–1552), to write against Luther and often did so himself to "root out the cursed Lutheran sects." Luther responded to all his opponents.

At the end of his life Duke Georg became a tragic figure. He had to accept the fact that the Reformation had made inroads within his state: after 1532 in the Freiberg domain of his brother Heinrich the Pious (1473–1541) and after 1537 in the Rochlitz area ruled by his widowed daughter-in-law Elisabeth (1502–57). Georg's efforts to defend his state against the Reformation after his death failed. His two sons died before their father. Later, Georg tried in his will to force his brother Heinrich, who was next in line, to the Catholic side, but negotiations with the Saxon estates over the will dragged on, and the issue was never resolved. In the spring of 1539 Heinrich the Pious assumed power and, at the funeral of his brother, made clear which denominational faith he intended to introduce into Albertine Saxony. On 6 July 1539 the first evangelical worship service was held in the Dresden Kreuzkirche.

In electoral (Ernestine) Saxony, after the turbulent early years, construction was begun on an evangelical state church under Friedrich the Wise's successors, his brother Johann the Constant (d. 1532) and Johann's son Johann Friedrich the Magnanimous (d. 1554). The duchy of Prussia, the first evangelical state—founded in 1525 by Albrecht of Brandenburg (1490–1568), grand master of the Teutonic Order—served as a model. The ruler was requested by Luther to maintain order in the church. In turn, from 1526 to 1530 electoral Saxony's church and school inspection, based on Melanchthon's 1528 *Instruction for Inspectors,* served as an example for other evangelical territories. The inspectors were to evaluate the life and teachings of the pastor and see that the nobility and the cities did not enrich themselves on church property. The inspections showed a shocking ignorance of religious matters among the pastors and members of the congregations. In 1529 Luther felt compelled to draw up the *Large Catechism* for pastors and the *Small Catechism* for the father of each household, both to be learned by heart. In the capital city of each district, pastors were installed as superintendents to oversee religious matters. Consistories were formed (the first in Wittenberg in 1539) to handle matters of ecclesiastical jurisdiction, such as matrimonial cases or complaints made against pastors. After 1539 the reorganization of the church hierarchy in Albertine Saxony proceeded simultaneously. For the use of the inspectors, Justus Jonas devised the "Heinrich Liturgy" (used in Duke Heinrich's territory), which became the official order of service.

Meanwhile, matters had come to a head in regard to the political situation of the empire. At the Diets of Speyer in 1526 and 1529, the Catholic princes renewed their decision to implement the Edict of Worms. The evangelical minority responded in 1529 with a formal protest, from which the name *Protestants* derives. The Diet of Augsburg in 1530 was a milestone in the development of the evangelical creed. At the request of the elector, Melanchthon worked out a position paper, *The Augsburg Confession (Confessio Augustana),* the first compilation of evangelical precepts. Thereupon, Eck, on orders of the emperor, produced a rebuttal *(Confutatio),* and the emperor regarded the case as settled. Because he had been pronounced an outlaw, Luther could not take part in the Augsburg proceedings. He watched events from the Coburg Castle and ridiculed the "parliament of crows and jackdaws," as he called it. Melanchthon's *Augsburg Confession* seemed too moderate for him, and he remarked, "I cannot tread so quietly and gently." In 1537 Luther strengthened the contents of the *Augsburg Confession* by issuing the *Schmalkald Articles,* which became a statement of faith of the Lutheran Church.

The Diet concluded without an agreement but with the emperor's threat to wage war against the evangelical princes if they did not submit. To protect themselves against this danger, they formed the Schmalkaldic League as a war alliance in February 1531. This league and the additional threat of danger from the Turks forced the emperor to agree to a truce. In the Nuremberg Truce of 1532 the Protestants were tacitly tolerated until a future council could be called. The council met again in 1545 in Trent, a town in the far south of the empire. It was a gathering of Catholics only, since the German Protestants refused to attend. Luther did not live to see the ensuing setbacks for the Reformation. He died on 18 February 1546 in Eisleben.

Because a solution could not be found through the Council of Trent, the emperor chose to enforce his power by waging war against the Protestant rebel princes (the Schmalkaldic War, 1546–47). During the war Duke Moritz of Saxony (d. 1553) came under a cloud. Although he firmly supported the development of the Reformation in Albertine Saxony, he was lured by the diplomacy of the Habsburgs and the promise of gaining electoral status and Ernestine Saxon territory. This promise, and the chance to reverse the 1485 partition of Saxony, prompted him to fight on the side of the emperor. Following the defeat of the Schmalkaldic League at the battle of Mühlberg in April 1547, the imperial Diet in 1548 issued the Augsburg Interim, which permitted the Protestants only two concessions: lay participation in the offering of communion and the marriage of priests. Otherwise, it required a return to the old doctrines and rites. Duke Moritz, because he had supported the Catholic emperor and won electoral status as a result, was scorned by the people as the "Judas of Meissen." He came under further pressure and had to implement the Augsburg Interim as imperial law even in his own territory. Playing for time, he asked his consulting theologians, particularly Melanchthon, to work out a less strict version, the Leipzig Articles. The articles conceded to the Catholic rites *adiaphora* (unimportant matters), such as the structure of the worship service, but held firm to the basic articles of evangelical doctrine, such as justification by faith.

The Leipzig Articles were never implemented. Instead, there began one of many internal disputes among the Protestants, which continued for several decades and reached a critical point in Saxony with crypto-Calvinism and the fall of the chancellor Nikolaus Krell (1550?–1601). This time, the Gnesio Lutherans, the "true Lutherans"—that is, Lutheran theologians such as Nikolaus von Amsdorf (1483–1565), Matthias Flacius Illyricus (1520–75), and their followers—criticized the "Philippists" (Philipp Melanchthon and his followers) for being too ready to compromise and rejected the Leipzig Articles as a "Leipzig Interim." The attacks they made in their campaign were clearly directed against Duke Moritz.

For personal reasons, but largely because of the repressive power and religious policy of the emperor, Duke Moritz changed sides, joined the north German evangelical princes (who were opposed to the emperor for the same reasons), and became their leader and the savior of Protestantism. Strengthened by a treaty with the French King Henry II (1519–59), Moritz took the field with the evangelical princes in a surprise attack against the emperor, who, however, escaped. On 2 August 1552 the evangelical princes formulated the Treaty of Passau, which led to the Religious Peace of Augsburg on 25 September 1555. The Peace of Augsburg recognized "those associated with the Augsburg Confession" and allowed them their religious independence.

The Reformation came to an end in Saxony with the General Articles issued in 1557 by Elector August I (d. 1586, brother and successor of Moritz). Along with Heinrich's Liturgy, the General Articles represent the first binding church legislation.

The Reformation, yielding to political pressure, relied on the holders of territorial power who had made it possible and assured its survival. As a result, there were as many legally independent state churches as there were political territories. The Religious Peace of Augsburg permitted only the sovereign rulers to select the religious denomination of their territory, under the principle *cuius regio, eius religio.* This religious decision by the prince was, therefore, of vital importance to his subjects. The state rulers and also the emperor, despite their apparent piety, used religion as a means to achieve their political goals. Famous examples of this were Henry IV's (1553–1610) conversion to Catholicism at the end of the century to become King of France

("Paris is worth a mass"), and the conversion of the Saxon elector August the Strong (Friedrich August I, d. 1733) to acquire the Polish crown. By then, subjects no longer had to change their religious affiliation to that of the ruler. Thus, Saxony has remained largely Lutheran to this day.

The Protestant states received permanent benefits in the improvement of their educational systems. Through their writings, Luther and Melanchthon appealed to the authorities to establish schools, including schools for girls. Melanchthon's reorganization of the University of Wittenberg was an example for all other Protestant universities, as were his widely circulated instruction books. The Latin schools were reformed and were closely connected with evangelical and humanist education. Melanchthon became the Praeceptor Germaniae. In 1543 Saxony established the basis for its own educational tradition with Elector Moritz's order to form the princely schools *(Fürstenschulen)* of St. Afra in Meissen, St. Marien in Pforta (Schulpforta near Naumburg), and St. Augustin in Grimma. These university-preparatory schools were attended by children of the princes and the nobility, as well as young people from various cities. They also provided scholarships for poor students.

The favorite art form of Protestantism was music. Luther himself favored a "singing church" and considered choral singing as important to the church experience as the sermon and communion. In his words, "To a good sermon belongs a good song." Where there was a shortage of German songs, Luther would compose his own, and today the evangelical church can thank him for some of its most beautiful hymns.

The Reformation divided Christendom into different denominations, with the Catholic Church no longer representing all Christians. The privileges and responsibilities of the individual in Reformation theology extended to, and caused changes in, the secular world of commerce, education, law, and personal conduct. Society was not completely secularized; belief in an active and omnipresent God remained central to late medieval and early Renaissance life. However, now the nature of that God and humanity's relation to him was open to multiple interpretations.

Detail, Illustration 33

Hans-Jürgen Sarfert

The Literature of Romanticism in Dresden

In European intellectual history, Romanticism was a direct reaction to the prescribed rules of reason of the Enlightenment. It was also a call for intellectual renewal that had evolved from the changes brought by the French Revolution that began in 1789. Romanticism was a group phenomenon, involving friendships among writers and literary circles. Intellectuals combined the demand for freedom with the elimination of the current literary standard and strengthened the imagination through sensitive expression. Romantic authors and artists wanted to revitalize what they thought of as the universal value concepts of the Middle Ages in Germany. Romanticism developed into a literary movement centered in the cities of Berlin, Heidelberg, and Jena and was also referred to in regional terms, as Rhine, Munich, or Swabian Romanticism.

Dresden as a Source of Artistic Inspiration

For a brief period Dresden was one of the centers of Romanticism. Because of the beauty of its countryside, Dresden has always been a place of inspiration for artists and musicians. The "Romantic School" was born in Dresden during the summer of 1798, when a group of Romantics brought recognition and attention to the *Sistine Madonna,* which the Dresden Royal Gallery had owned since 1754. This was an altar painting from the church of the San Sisto Benedictine Monastery in Piacenza, Italy, which had been donated to the monastery by Pope Julius II. It was acquired for the Saxon capital city by Elector Friedrich August II for 20,000 gold ducats (approximately US$200,000 today). This painting by Raphael Santi (1483–1520) became a world-famous work of art. The American poet Henry Miles (1824–71) wrote in his poem "San Sisto" that the Madonna had made Dresden a "Holy City."

The young men and women who came to Dresden during the summer of 1798 to widen their horizons were unusually gifted and sensitive individuals. They were the group of Romantics from Jena, who had first gathered at the Pillnitz home of the Saxon privy councilor Ludwig Emanuel Ernst and his wife Charlotte. This group included five prominent authors: Friedrich Schlegel, August Wilhelm and Caroline Schlegel, Friedrich von Hardenberg, and Friedrich Wilhelm Joseph Schelling.

Friedrich Schlegel (1772–1829) was already familiar with this center of artistic riches through his stay in Dresden from January 1794 to the summer of 1796. He had devoted this period to an exhaustive study of the history of classical literature, the theory of literature, and the philosophy of history. Schlegel always emphasized the profound influence these two and a half years in Dresden had had on his literary life.

His brother, August Wilhelm Schlegel (1767–1845), professor of literature and philology and inspired translator of Shakespeare's plays, had also decided to move to Dresden in August 1796, although he feared that he would be subject to the city's conservatism. He was accompanied by his wife, Caroline (1763–1809), one of the most interesting women of the Romantic period and an accomplished letter writer.

Von Hardenberg (1772–1801) of nearby Freiberg is perhaps best known as Novalis (cultivator of new land), as he called himself. This profound lyric poet of great melodic sadness was also a systematic and mystical thinker. Schelling (1775–1854) became a professor in Jena at age twenty-three and had already published basic works in natural philosophy.

These five authors met in Dresden, the "Florence of the North," on 25–26 August 1798, to view and discuss works in the classical collection of the Japanese Palace (once the location of what is now the Saxon State Library), where torchlights illuminated the stone contours of the building. In the art gallery of the Johanneum, a three-story Renaissance building constructed in 1586 at the Neuen Markt, they studied the gestures and expressions portrayed in the fabled paintings of Claude Lorrain, Jacob van Ruisdael, Hans Holbein, Salvator Rosa, Correggio (Antonio Allegri), and Giorgione. Kneeling before the *Sistine Madonna,* the five authors poetically consecrated it as "the acme of human creativity."

In their discussions, they emphasized authentic experience and the early Romantic world of contemplation. The discussions culminated in the poetic-philosophic dialogue *Die Gemählde* (The Paintings), written by August Wilhelm and Caroline Schlegel and published the following year in the journal *Athenaeum. Die Gemählde* was the basic document and *Athenaeum* the most important publication for formulating the theory of early romanticism. The theory grew out of that overwhelming experience in the Dresden gallery.

Influence on American and British Literary History

The influence of the Schlegel brothers on American literary history has been documented by Ernst Behler, the German-American specialist in German Romanticism at the University of Washington. As one of the leading scholars of their manuscripts, he published *The Writings of the Schlegel Brothers* in 1983. August Wilhelm's literary history was translated into English in 1815. The first American edition appeared in 1833. It is known to have influenced the literature of the American writer Edgar Allan Poe (1809–49). As early as 1812 the Philadelphia journal *Port Folio* referred to Schlegel's Vienna lectures "On Dramatic Art and Literature" (which had been published in Heidelberg in 1809–11). An English translation of Friedrich's *History of Old and New Literature* (Vienna, 1815), which advanced new theories in German literary criticism, appeared in Philadelphia in 1818. By 1833 scholarly discussions of the Schlegel brothers appeared frequently in literary journals, particularly in the *American Monthly Review.* They were respected, cited, and credited with stimulating interest in aesthetic concepts in American literary criticism.

Strong ties also existed between the German and English Romanticists. Thomas Carlyle (1795–1881), the great English historian and writer, valued German culture and translated the works of many German writers for English-speaking audiences. In 1829 he wrote a thoughtful and stimulating essay on Novalis, which made a lasting impression on Anglo-American audiences. Before the complete translation was published in 1842, *The New Yorker* published in 1839, on its title page, a translation of the "Weinlied" from Novalis's novel *Heinrich von Ofterdingen.* The Americans Henry Wadsworth Longfellow (1807–82) and Poe showed a strong interest in Novalis's writing, establishing an awareness of him among a small literary public. Finally, the "Blaue Blume" became a popular symbol of the Romantic concept of happiness in Henry van Dyke's (1852–1933) *Blue Flower* (1902), a paraphrased version of the first dream in *Heinrich von Ofterdingen.*

Romantics in the Library

During the eighteenth century, the Court Library in Dresden developed into a renowned European cultural institution. The Romantic writers eagerly consulted its valuable resources during their visits to Dresden. The lending records from 1797 to 1803 show that the Schlegel brothers visited the library on 3 July 1798 and that Friedrich borrowed the *Göttingische Museum,* while his brother delved into *Anderson's Collections of English Poets* (London, 1795). Several days later Friedrich, who was studying the works of Petrarch, borrowed the *Obras Livicas* by another humanist, the Spaniard Diego Hurtado de Mendoza (1503–75).

On 10 August 1799 Novalis visited the library for the first time. He made frequent visits thereafter in 1800 and 1801, at least nine in all, revealing his interest in the Greek tragedians Aeschylus and Sophocles; the theosophical writings of the Silesian mystic Jakob Böhme (1575–1624), whose search for God moved him deeply; and the poems of the prolific *Meistersinger* Hans Sachs (1494–1576). On 20 January 1801, deathly ill, the twenty-nine-year-old Novalis left Dresden, but four days later he returned Tiberius Cavallo's *Treatment of the Theoretical and Practical Knowledge of Electricity* (Leipzig, 1783) to the library, an indication of his interest in the natural sciences.

Another regular user of the library was Ludwig Tieck (1773–1853), a Romantic writer with a highly developed sense of fantasy, who moved easily and skillfully in all literary genres. He lived in Dresden from 1801 to 1803 and later from 1819 to 1841 as councilor and drama critic. He became a central figure in the literary life of the city. During his first stay in Dresden, Tieck made no fewer than twenty-five visits to the library.

Influence of Dresden on Intellectuals

Heinrich von Kleist (1777–1811) was also living in Dresden. A writer of international literary standing, he did not fit the aesthetic system of classical harmony fostered by Goethe and Schiller. He saw the entanglements and fatalism of human existence in a puzzling world. Kleist's short life was dominated by this view of reality in which he sought in vain the realm of the ideal. Yet in Dresden, where he found friends and understanding, he spent a happy period from 31 August 1807 to 29 April 1809. Earlier, in 1801, he had written from Paris: "What's happening in my dear Dresden?" When he came to Dresden, he met a remarkable group of prolific intellectuals. Adam Müller (1779–1829), an expert in many subjects, was giving brilliant lectures on German science and literature. He had written the introduction to Kleist's *Amphitryon.*

Many unpublished manuscripts were circulated among this group. The journal *Phoebus,* founded by Müller on 17 December 1807, called for "popularizing all art works of the most contradictory forms and as varied as they can be," to stimulate the advancement of ideas. The intention was to test and promote directly and radically the early Romantic ideal of unity from multiplicity, as in the synthesizing of opposing texts. After its initial success, the journal ceased publication in February 1809 after only nine issues, because of strong competition and a shortage of funds. Many of the great literary men of the day, from Goethe to Christoph Martin Wieland, refused to contribute, causing a decline in circulation. Nevertheless, *Phoebus* was the most important literary journal focusing upon the aesthetic debate to be published in Dresden. Its particular value lay in Kleist's original contributions. *Phoebus* published the powerful Robert-Guiskard Fragment, the draft of a play that Kleist intended as the greatest drama of all time. Other important drafts of his pioneering creations are known largely through this publication.

Although he worked in Dessau, Wilhelm Müller (1794–1827) frequently visited Dresden. This Romantic folk writer composed simple, lyrical poems that won wide acceptance, such as "Am Brunnen vor dem Tore," "Das Wandern ist des Müllers Lust," and "Ich hört ein Bächlein rauschen." His lyrical song cycles, such as *Die schöne Müllerin* and *Die Winterreise,* became the greatest songs of composer Franz Schubert (1797–1828), the last master of the Viennese classical school. These unexcelled compositions embraced the content and mood of Müller's poems.

In a letter of 4 April 1824, Müller wrote about a trip to Dresden, "This visit has already become an annual necessity for me." Two weeks later, he wrote further, "I cannot stand to be away from Dresden longer than a year." He loved the cultural life of this city, where he had friends such as Tieck and the composer Carl Maria von Weber (1786–1826), a master of Romantic music. Müller dedicated the second collection of his *Waldhorn* songs to Weber. The founders of the Dresden Choral Society honored this young poet. During his numerous visits to the city, he always used the resources of the Royal Public Library, especially while working on his encyclopedic fourteen-volume *Library of Seventeenth-century German Writers* (1822).

At the library Müller had close contacts with Friedrich Adolf Ebert (1791–1834), who since 1814 had been heavily involved in efforts to develop the theoretical and scientific basis of library science. His work *Die Bildung des Bibliothekars* (1820) is still considered one of the standard authorities in the history of library science. In 1823 when Ebert accepted the offer to go to Wolfenbüttel to take charge of the library of Gotthold Ephraim Lessing (1729–81), the highly respected philosopher of the Enlightenment, Müller would have liked to take his place in Dresden and wrote, "May my deepest wish come true." His wish did come true: Dresden became Müller's second home and played a crucial role in his development as a poet. Today the International Wilhelm Müller Society preserves his work.

In late autumn of 1828 Friedrich Schlegel came to Dresden for the last time. While there, he gave public lectures and wrote a summary of his philosophy of life. From 25 March to 31 May he had lectured in Vienna on the philosophy of life and delivered eighteen lectures on the philosophy of history. These were challenging confrontations with the theories of the classical philosopher Georg Wilhelm Friedrich Hegel (1770–1831). On 5 December 1828 Schlegel began a series of lectures at the Hotel de Pologne in Dresden, where Adam Müller had also lectured. His topic was the philosophy of language and words. He was working on a universal system of Christian philosophy when, on 11 January 1829, he suffered a heart attack while reading the manuscript of his next lecture. He died within a few hours. The Dresden manuscripts were sent to Vienna on orders of the Austrian chancellor Metternich (1773–1859), who had known and liked Schlegel. Schlegel was buried in the Catholic cemetery in Dresden. Upon receiving news of his death, Adam Müller, coeditor of *Phoebus,* suffered a stroke and died.

The young Friedrich Schlegel had once said in a moment of enthusiasm, "My feelings of youth were first awakened in beautiful Dresden, where I first saw true works of art." In the end he returned to the city forever.

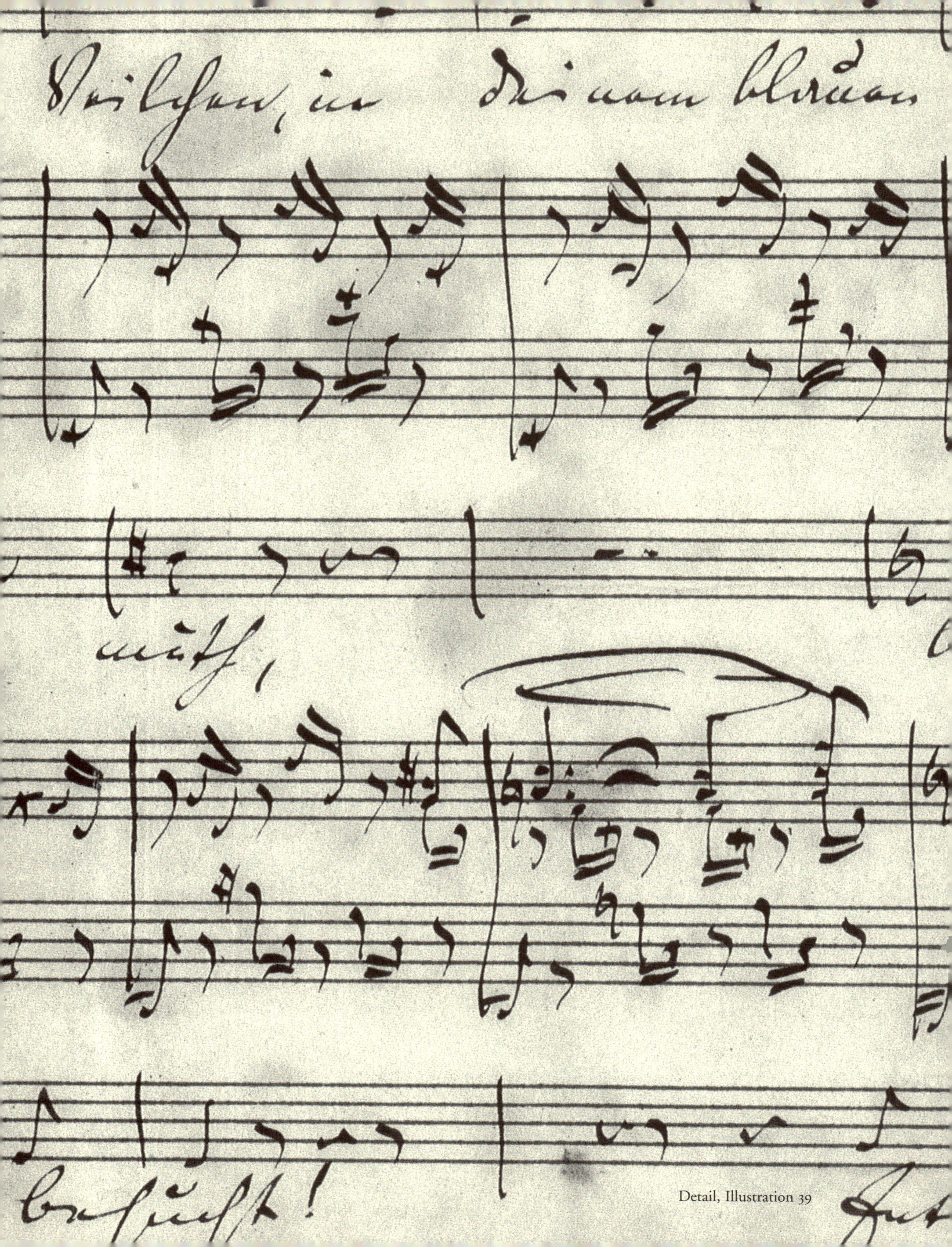

Detail, Illustration 39

Ortrun Landmann

Music in Saxony

The history of music in Saxony is among the richest and most dynamic in Germany, perhaps in Europe. Particularly noteworthy are Dresden's 770-year-old Kreuzchor, originally founded to train choristers for church altar services, and Leipzig's 740-year-old Thomanerchor, as well as the Staatskapelle of Dresden and the Leipzig Gewandhaus Orchestra. Founded in 1548 by Elector Moritz to accompany church services, the Staatskapelle is the oldest continually existing orchestra of court origin and is considered one of the leading European orchestras today. The Gewandhaus Orchestra, founded in 1743, is the oldest continually existing civic orchestra in Europe. The international acclaim these institutions have received is the result of the strong support of music both within and outside the church throughout Saxony and of a rich tradition of instrument making, especially in the Vogtland region of southwestern Saxony.

Music and the Schools

For centuries music education was emphasized in both the Latin schools and the parochial schools of the Evangelical Lutheran Church. In addition to the large city schools of Dresden, Leipzig, Zwickau, Freiberg, and other cities, there were three so-called *Fürstenschulen* (princely schools), Meissen, Grimma, and Pforta, which were established after the Reformation by the Saxon electors on confiscated monastic estates. Pforta became widely known through the publication of the motet collection, *Florilegium Portense.* Part 1 of the collection appeared in 1618, part 2 in 1621; numerous copies of both parts are still in existence today, for example, in the New York Public Library and the Library of Congress. Original music manuscripts of the St. Augustin School in Grimma, including several codices of musical compositions from the St. Afra School in Meissen, have been preserved and are today part of the holdings of the Saxon State Library.

Just as the *Florilegium Portense* indicates the broad scope of the music repertoire in the city and princely schools, the Grimma Collection demonstrates how important the music centers of Leipzig and Dresden became for these schools. Today, musicologists recognize how beneficial these manuscripts were for the musical development of the St. Thomas Church before Bach's arrival in Leipzig in 1723. Without this collection of manuscripts, many of the earlier works of composers such as Johann Rosenmüller, Johann David Heinichen, and Georg Philipp Telemann, who lived temporarily in Leipzig, would not have survived.

Music in Leipzig

In Leipzig, musical life for centuries was centered in the city's churches and university. Liturgical music reached its height in the work and influence of Johann Sebastian Bach, cantor of St. Thomas Church and director of music for Leipzig from 1723 to 1750. After his appointment as cantor, Bach composed five complete cycles of cantatas for the church calendar, containing approximately sixty cantatas each, for a total of almost three hundred sacred works, a repertoire unparalleled in Leipzig's musical history.

Leipzig was also known for its Collegium Musicum, founded by Telemann and directed by Bach in 1729. Such groups were voluntary associations of professional musicians and university students that gave weekly public concerts. In this way, many an aspiring lawyer or theologian discovered during his studies at Leipzig that his real vocation was music. A seventeenth-century example is Heinrich Schütz. Eighteenth-century examples include Johann David Heinichen, who later became Hofkapellmeister of the Dresden Hofkapelle; Johann Friedrich Fasch, later Hofkapellmeister in Zerbst; Georg Philipp Telemann, who became a conductor in Frankfurt am Main and Hamburg; and the Dresden concert-master Johann Georg Pisendel. Several of Bach's successors as music director at the St. Thomas Church were also graduates of law and theology from Leipzig University. Among the nineteenth-century graduates were the composers Heinrich Marschner and Carl Gottlieb Reißiger, who were later in Dresden, as was Robert Schumann.

Music in Dresden

In the capital city of Dresden, the Hofkapelle had such high standing that the other musical groups in Saxony could not seriously compete with it, although some of them were also excellent. When the Saxon electors were invited to the Reichstag in Berlin, they took along their celebrated Hofkapelle. It participated in festivals, weddings, and state occasions, events that were accompanied by sports tournaments, lavish opera productions, and processions in fancy costumes.

The Hofkapelle also played regularly at the court worship services. It had been founded in 1548 as the earliest Lutheran (court) ensemble, under the leadership of church music director and Hofkapellmeister Johann Walter. When Elector Friedrich August I (August the Strong, d. 1733) converted to Catholicism in 1697 in order to become king of Poland, some members left the Hofkapelle for religious reasons, since the ensemble would now be integrated into the Catholic worship services. At the same time the old organizational form of the Hofkapelle that had developed under Schütz was changed to a more modern form. Obsolete instruments gave way to new ones that are still in use today.

Essential to this early development was the international character of the Hofkapelle. From its beginning, it had drawn conductors, as well as members, from Italy, the Netherlands, and England. When the electors traveled to other countries, such as Italy or France, they adopted new musical developments that they observed in their journeys. In 1685 Johann Georg III (d. 1691) brought back from a trip a prima donna whom he had lured away from the service of the duke of Mantua. This represented a dramatic change for the Hofkapelle, since until this time female stage roles had been played and sung by men (either in falsetto or in the naturally high voices of castrati).

Outside the church the Hofkapelle's vocalists and instrumentalists participated increasingly in court concerts and theater performances, such as *Daphne* by Martin Opitz and Heinrich Schütz in 1627. Opera performances were especially well received in Dresden, as they are to this day. From 1662 to 1816 opera was sung almost exclusively in Italian at the Dresden court; performances in French were rare, and German performances took place only after the German Opera opened in 1817. Italian opera in Dresden reached its zenith under the direction of Johann Adolf Hasse (1734–63). The nineteenth-century German Opera, best known as the Hofoper, had two outstanding periods influenced respectively by the tenure as Hofkapellmeister of Carl Maria von Weber (1817–26) and Richard Wagner (1842–49).

For centuries the brilliant reputation of the Dresden Hofkapelle attracted renowned soloists, such as violinists Johann Georg Pisendel, Antonio Rolla, and Karol Lipinski; cellists Friedrich Dotzauer, Friedrich August Kummer, and Friedrich Grützmacher; flutists Pierre-Gabriel Buffardin, Johann Joachim Quantz, and Anton Bernhard Fürstenau; and oboists Johann Christian Richter and Antonio and Carlo Besozzi. The Dresden musicians were also sought-after teachers. Great works on music instruction were written by the conductors Giovanni Andrea Bontempi (Dresden, 1660), Christoph Bernhard (a work that survives in a seventeenth-century manuscript), and Johann David Heinichen. Heinichen's *Basso Continuo in Music* (Dresden, 1728) is still considered the standard work on the subject. Other important instructional works include Quantz's *On Playing the Flute* (published in Berlin in 1752, but mainly reflecting Dresden orchestra practice) and Moritz Fürstenau's still unsurpassed *History of the Theater and Music at the Dresden Court* (1861–62), the earliest local history of such scope.

The conductor Michael Praetorius had relied on the instruments of the Dresden Hofkapelle in his description of common and rare musical instruments for his *Syntagma musicum* (1615–20). Similarly, in 1910–11 a group from the Dresden Hofkapelle published a more general three-volume work, *Musical Instruments in Word and Picture,* edited by E. Teuchert and E. W. Haupt.

Saxony's Music Publishing Industry and Depositories

A lively music-publishing industry developed as a result of the musical works produced in Saxony. Leipzig, with its long-standing tradition of book publishing and book fairs, gradually became the center of music publishing. Such famous publishers as Breitkopf & Härtel and C. F. Peters were located in Leipzig. Although there was considerable competition among the well-schooled Dresden court copyists in the field of hand-copied music, Leipzig in the eighteenth century achieved a leading position in music publishing and it continued to enlarge its dominance of the market until the end of the nineteenth century. There was hardly a publishing house from Russia to the United States that did not have its musical works printed in Leipzig.

This prodigious output of hand-copied and printed music posed a problem for storage and cataloging. For this reason, during the nineteenth century large scholarly libraries became depositories for historical music material. Often the works had passed through the hands of private collectors and were donated to or purchased by the libraries.

In 1816 the noted librarian Friedrich Adolf Ebert established a Music Department at the Royal Public Library in Saxony, now the Saxon State Library. A special catalog lists the impressive original collection, which was later enhanced by donations of entire collections. In 1890 the library received several music collections from Saxon churches, city archives, and schools; these were followed in 1897 by the splendid private music collection of the Saxon kings, dating primarily from the eighteenth and nineteenth centuries. Unfortunately, the Hofkapelle's archives from the sixteenth and seventeenth centuries, which included music materials by Heinrich Schütz written in his own hand, were destroyed in the Prussian bombardment of Dresden in 1760.

In the twentieth century the collection was further enlarged by music materials from the royal, church, and opera collections; the Grimma and Zittau collections; and the Annaberg choirbooks. During World War II bombs destroyed most of the contemporary music collection of the Saxon State Library. After the war, however, the library once again began to collect the work of contemporary composers. The primary emphasis continues to be on original manuscripts by Saxon composers and on compositions that either received their premiere in Dresden or have other ties to Dresden or Saxony. As long as the library maintains this high standard for collecting Saxony's musical heritage, its renowned position in the world of music will be secure.

Bibliography

Compiled by Eberhard Stimmel

*Note: Entries for titles held by the Library of Congress include the Library of Congress call number in **bold-face** type.*

Literature about the Saxon State Library

Aus der Arbeit der Sächsischen Landesbibliothek 1956–1965. Edited by Burghard Burgemeister. Dresden: Sächsische Landesbibliothek, 1966. 152 pp. **z802.d77 a9**

Aus der Arbeit der Sächsischen Landesbibliothek: Zehnjahrbericht 1966–1975. Edited by Burghard Burgemeister. Dresden: Sächsische Landesbibliothek, 1977. 286 pp. **z803.d73 1977**

Bollert, Martin. *Jahresbericht der Sächsischen Landesbibliothek 1930–1935.* Dresden: Sächsische Landesbibliothek, 1936. 64 pp.

Deckert, Helmut. *Katalog der Inkunabeln der Sächsischen Landesbibliothek zu Dresden.* Zentralblatt für Bibliothekswesen, 80. Leipzig: Harrassowitz, 1957. 255 pp., portrait, facs. **z671.c39 b no. 80**

Deckert, Helmut. *Maya-Handschrift der Sächsischen Landesbibliothek Dresden: Geschichte und Bibliographie.* Berlin: Akademie-Verlag, 1962. 86 pp., color facs. (in pocket). **f1435.3.p6 d4**

Ebert, Friedrich Adolf. *Geschichte und Beschreibung der Königlichen Öffentlichen Bibliothek zu Dresden.* Leipzig: Brockhaus, 1822. xviii + 358 pp. **z802.d77e**

Ermisch, Hubert Georg. *Das Japanische Palais in Dresden-Neustadt.* Geschichtliche Wanderfahrten, 40. Dresden: C. Heinrich, 1935. 39 pp.

Falkenstein, Karl. *Beschreibung der Königlichen Öffentlichen Bibliothek zu Dresden.* Dresden: Walthersche Hofbuchhandlung, 1839. 887 pp. **z802.d7 c3 1839**

Führer durch das Buchmuseum. Edited by Christian Alschner. Dresden: Sächsische Landesbibliothek, 1979. **n6865.d39**

Goetze, Johann Christian. *Die Merckwürdigkeiten der Königlichen Bibliotheck zu Dresden.* Dresden: Walther, 1743. 562 pp.

Hantzsch, Viktor. *Die Landkartenbestände der Königlichen Öffentlichen Bibliothek zu Dresden.* Zentralblatt für Bibliothekswesen, 28. Leipzig: Harrassowitz, 1904. 146 pp.

Jahresbericht der Königlichen Öffentlichen Bibliothek (ab 1918 der Sächsischen Landesbibliothek) 1910–1929. Jährlich wechselnde Seitenzahl. Dresden: Sächsische Landesbibliothek, 1911–30.

Katalog der Handschriften der Sächsischen Landesbibliothek zu Dresden. 5 vols. Dresden: Sächsische Landesbibliothek, 1979–86.

Neubert, Hermann. *Zur Geschichte der Sächsischen Landesbibliothek.* Leipzig: Harrassowitz, 1936. 61 pp., ill. (including plans, plates). **z802.d77n**

PETZHOLD, JULIUS. *Dresdens Bibliotheken: Ein Wegweiser für Fremde und Einheimische.* Dresden: Arnoldische Buchhandlung, 1846. 108 pp.

Sächsische Landesbibliothek. *Die Wettiner als Förderer von Kunst und Wissenschaft: Handschriften, Stiche, Zeichnungen, Druckwerke aus dem Bestand der Sächsischen Landesbibliothek Dresden: Ausstellung vom 1. Februar bis 30. Juni 1989, Sächsische Landesbibliothek Dresden.* Edited by Katrin Nitzschke. Dresden: Sächsische Landesbibliothek, 1989. 35 pp., ill. **NX550.6.A3 S294 1989**

Sächsische Landesbibliothek 1976–1985, Die. Edited by Burghard Burgemeister. Dresden: Sächsische Landesbibliothek, 1987. 176 pp. **Z803.S23 S24 1977**

Sächsische Landesbibliothek Dresden: 1556–1956; Festschrift zum 400-jährigen Bestehen. Leipzig: Sächsische Landesbibliothek, 1956. 298 pp.

SLB-Kurier: Nachrichten aus der Sächsischen Landesbibliothek. Dresden: Direktor der Sächsischen Landesbibliothek, 1987—. Ill. **Z803.S23 S58**

Über die Arbeitsteilung im Dresdner Bibliothekswesen: Untersuchungen zu ihrer Geschichte und Perspektive; wissenschaftliche Festveranstaltung anläßlich des 425-jährigen Bestehens der Sächsischen Landesbibliothek, Dresden, 15.10.1981. Edited by Burghard Burgemeister. Dresden: Sächsische Landesbibliothek, 1982. 108 pp., 3 leaves of plates, 3 ill. (color). **Z803.S23.U27 1982**

Literature about Dresden

BADER, KARIN, ed. *Dresden in 144 Bildern.* Leer: Rautenberg, 1991. 144 ill. **DD901.D74 D73 1991**

BERGANDER, GÖTZ. *Dresden im Luftkrieg: Vorgeschichte, Zerstörung, Folgen.* Weimar: Böhlau, 1994. 435 pp., ill., maps. **D757.9.D7B47 1994**

Bibliographie zur Geschichte der Stadt Dresden. Edited by Historische Komission der Sächsischen Akademie der Wissenschaften and Sächsischen Landesbibliothek. 5 vols. Dresden: Sächsische Landesbibliothek, 1981–84. **Z2244.D7 B53 1981**

DIECKMANN, FRIEDRICH. *Dresdner Ansichten: Spaziergänge und Erkundungen.* Frankfurt am Main: Insel-Verlag, 1995. 194 pp., ill.

Dresden: Ein Reisebuch. Edited by Katrin Nitzschke. Frankfurt am Main: Insel-Verlag, 1993. 293 pp.

Dresden in alten Ansichtskarten. Frankfurt am Main: Umschau-Verlag, 1976. 128 pp., many ill. (some color). **DD901.D74 D74**

Dresden: Stadt der Fürsten, Stadt der Künstler. Edited by Katrin Nitzschke and Lothar Koch. Bergisch Gladbach: Lübbe, 1992. 256 pp., ill. (some color). **DD901.D75 D75 1992**

GRETZSCHEL, MATTHIAS. *Die Dresdner Frauenkirche.* Hamburg: Ellert & Richter, 1994. 231 pp., ill.

LÖFFLER, FRITZ. *Das alte Dresden: Geschichte seiner Bauten.* Leipzig: Seemann, 1994. 504 pp.

MARX, HARALD. *Dresden.* Würzburg: Stütz, 1992. 144 pp., ill. (color). **N6886.D7 K37 1994**

Museen in Dresden: Ein Führer durch 42 Museen und Sammlungen. Edited by Manfred Bachmann and Hans Prescher. Leipzig: Edition Leipzig, 1991. 326 pp., ill. (some color), maps. **AM51.D7M88 1991**

...Oder Dresden: Fotos, Dokumente und Texte einer Ausstellung 40 Jahre nach der Zerstörung der Stadt. Edited by Winfried Werner. Dresden: Fischer, 1991. 111 pp., ill.

QUINGER, HEINZ. *Dresden und Umgebung: Geschichte und Kunst der sächsischen Hauptstadt.* Cologne: DuMont, 1993. 400 pp. **DD901.D74Q56 1993**

Stadtlexikon Dresden A–Z. Edited by Folke Stimmel et al. Dresden: Verlag der Kunst, 1994. 511 pp., ill. (some color), bibliography, index. **DD901.D73 S73 1994**

Verbrannt bis zur Unkenntlichkeit: Die Zerstörung Dresdens 1945. Edited by Stadtmuseum Dresden. Altenburg: DZA Verlag für Kultur und Wissenschaft, 1994. 161 pp., ill.

Literature about Saxony

Albert Herzog zu Sachsen: Die Wettiner in Lebensbildern. Graz: Styria, 1995.

Blaschke, Karlheinz. *Der Fürstenzug zu Dresden: Denkmal und Geschichte des Hauses Wettin.* Leipzig: Urania, 1991. 224 pp., ill. (chiefly color). **DD801.S357 B55 1991**

Blaschke, Karlheinz. *Geschichte Sachsens im Mittelalter.* Munich: Beck, 1990. 397 pp., ill. **DD801.S361 B55 1990**

Czok, Karl. *Am Hofe August des Starken.* Stuttgart: Deutsche Verlags-Anstalt, 1990. 178 pp., ill. **DD801.S395 C95 1990**

Delau, Reinhard. *August der Starke: Bilder einer Zeit.* Halle: Mitteldeutscher Verlag, 1989. 247 pp., ill. (some color). **DD801.S95 D45 1989**

Dohmann, Albrecht. *Sachsen.* Leipzig: Edition Leipzig, 1993. 469 pp., ill. **N6881.D74 1993**

Engelhardt, Heiderose. *Sachsen: Kunstfahrten zwischen Leipzig, Dresden und Chemnitz.* Munich: Bucher, 1993. 224 pp., ill. (color). **N6881.E54 1993**

Fellmann, Walter. *Sachsens letzter König, Friedrich August III.* Berlin: Koehler & Amelang, 1992. 263 pp., ill. **DD801.S44 F45 1992**

Gerlach, Siegfried, ed. *Sachsen: Eine politische Landeskunde.* Stuttgart: Kohlhammer, 1993. 291 pp. **JN4836.S23 1993**

Gretzschel, Matthias. *Sachsen.* Hamburg: Ellert & Richter, 1993. 96 pp., many ill. (chiefly color). **DD801.S34 G75 1993**

Hansmann, Wilfried. *Im Glanz des Barock: ein Begleiter zu den Bauwerken August des Starken und Friedrich des Großen.* Cologne: DuMont, 1992. 300 pp., ill. (some color) **NA1086.D7 H36 1992**

Jahrhundert der Reformation in Sachsen, Das: Festgabe zum 450-jährigen Bestehen der Evangelisch-Lutherischen Landeskirche Sachsens: Im Auftrag der Arbeitsgemeinschaft für Sächsische Kirchengeschichte. Edited by Helmar Junghans. Berlin: Evangelische Verlagsanstalt, 1989. 261 pp., ill., including 32 pp. of plates. **BR358.S3 J34 1989**

Mitten in Europa: Der Freistaat Sachsen und seine Region. Edited by Sächsische Staatskanzlei. Wiesbaden: Gabler, 1991. 143 pp., ill. **HC287.S3 M58 1991**

Naumann, Günter. *Sächsische Geschichte in Daten.* Berlin: Koehler & Amelang, 1991. 302 pp. **DD801.S352 N38 1991**

Pleticha, Heinrich. *Kulturlandschaft Sachsen.* Freiburg im Breisgau: Herder, 1992. 198 pp., ill. (some color). **DD801.S34 P55 1992**

Sachsen: Historische Landeskunde Mitteldeutschlands. Edited by Hermann Heckmann. Würzburg: Weidlich, 1991. 275 pp., ill.

Wissenschafts- und Universitätsgeschichte in Sachsen im 18. und 19. Jahrhundert: Nationale und internationale Wechselwirkung und Ausstrahlung: Beiträge des internationalen Kolloquiums zum 575. Jahr der Universitätsgründung am 26. und 27. November 1984 in Leipzig. Edited by Karl Czok. Berlin: Akademie-Verlag, 1987. 242 pp., ill. (including plates). **LA747.W57 1987**

ZIMMERMANN, INGO. *Sachsens Markgrafen, Kurfürsten und Könige: Die Wettiner in der meissnisch-sächsischen Geschichte.* Berlin: Berliner Verlags-Anstalt Union, 1990. 141 pp., ill. **DD801.S357 Z56 1990**

Other Works of Interest

BLASCHKE, KARLHEINZ, et al., eds. *Freistaat Sachsen stellt sich vor.* Dresden: Sächsische Landeszentrale für politische Bildung, 1991. 74 pp., ill., maps. **DD801.S35 F47 1991**

BLICKLE, PETER. *Die Revolution von 1525.* Munich and Vienna: Oldenbourg, 1981. 326 pp., ill. **DD182.B6 1981**

BREUL, KARL HERRMANN. *The Romantic Movement in German Literature.* Cambridge: Heffer, 1927. xiv + 506 pp. **PT1172.B7**

CHRISTENSEN, CARL C. *Princes and Propaganda: Electoral Saxon Art of the Reformation.* Kirksville, Mo.: Sixteenth Century Journal Publishers, 1992. viii + 149 pp., ill. **ND1317.2.C47 1992**

GRIMM, REINHOLD, et al., eds. *Romanticism Today: Friedrich Schlegel, Novalis, E. T. A. Hoffmann, Ludwig Tieck.* Bonn: Inter Nationes, 1973. 90 pp., ill. **PT362.R595**

HENNENBERG, FRITZ. *The Leipzig Gewandhaus Orchestra.* Leipzig: Edition Leipzig, 1962. 101 pp., ill., portrait, facs. **ML280.8.L3 G26**

HOFMANN, ERNA HEDWIG. *The Dresden Kreuz Chor.* Leipzig: Edition Leipzig, 1962. 98 pp., ill., phonograph record (2 sides, 7 in., 45 rpm) laid in. **ML280.8.D7 K733**

JÄGER, ECKHARD. *Leipzig im Spiegel alter Graphik: Eine Ikonographie zur Geschichte des Leipziger Stadtbildes und seiner Bauten vom 16.–19. Jahrhundert.* Darmstadt: Blaschke, 1970. 104, 18 pp., ill. (6 in pocket). **Z2244.L5 J33**

JOHN, HANS. *Der Dresdner Kreuzchor und seine Kantoren.* Berlin: Evangelische Verlagsanstalt, 1982. 176 pp., ill., including 32 pp. of plates. **ML2929.J64 1982**

JOHST, HUGO, ed. *Leipzig in alten Ansichtskarten.* Frankfurt am Main: Flechsig, 1978. 103 pp., ill. **DD901.L54 L525**

KLEIN, THOMAS. *Der Kampf um die zweite Reformation in Kursachsen, 1586–1591.* Cologne: Böhlau, 1962. x + 220 pp. **BR358.S3 K55 1962**

KOBUCH, AGATHA. *Zensur und Aufklärung in Kursachsen: Ideologische Strömungen und politische Meinungen zur Zeit der sächsisch-polnischen Union (1697–1763).* Weimar: Böhlaus Nachfolger, 1988. 298 pp. **CD1280. A35 Vol. 12**

KOENIGSBERGER, HELMUT GEORG. *Luther: A Profile.* London: Macmillan, 1973. xxii + 234 pp. **BR326.K575 1973b**

LAUX, KARL. *The Dresden Staatskapelle.* Leipzig: VEB Edition, 1964. 125 pp., ill. **ML1729.8.D72 M843**

Leipzig, aus Vergangenheit und Gegenwart. Edited by Museum für Geschichte der Stadt Leipzig. Leipzig: Fachbuchverlag, 1984. 275 pp., ill. **DD901.L55 L37 1984**

LINDSAY, THOMAS MARTIN. *Luther and the German Reformation.* Freeport, N.Y.: Books for Libraries Press, 1970. xii + 300 pp. **BR325.L48 1970**

OBERMAN, HEIKO AUGUSTINUS. *Luther: Man between God and the Devil.* Translated by Eileen Walliser-Schwarzbart. New Haven: Yale University Press, 1989. 380 pp., ill. **BR325.O2713 1989**

PIETZSCH, GERHARD. *Sachsen als Musikland.* Dresden: Verlag Heimatwerk Sachsen, 1938. 96 pp., ill. (including music plates and facs.), portrait. **ML280.P5 S2**

RABE, HORST. *Reichsbund und Interim: Die Verfassungs- und Religionspolitik Karls V. und der Reichstag von Augsburg 1547/1548.* Cologne and Vienna: Böhlau, 1917. 496 pp. **DD180.R17**

Schanze, Helmut, ed. *Romantik-Handbuch.* Stuttgart: A. Kroner, 1994. 802 pp. **PT361.R616 1994**

Schilling, Heinz. *Aufbruch und Krise: Deutschland, 1517–1648.* Berlin: Siedler, 1988. 507 pp., ill., maps. **DD176.S3 1988**

Semper, Gottfried, ed. *Königliche Hoftheater zu Dresden.* Introduction by Harold Hammer-Schenk. Braunschweig: Vieweg, 1986. Portrait. **NA6840.G352 475 1986**

Splendors of Dresden, The. New York: Newsweek, 1979. **N2280.S67**

Steindorf, Eberhard. *Die Staatskapelle Dresden.* Leipzig: Bibliographisches Institut, 1987. 91 pp., ill. **ML1229.8.D72S77 1987**

Steude, Wolfram. *Musikgeschichte Dresdens in Umrissen.* Dresden: Sächsische Landesbibliothek, 1978. 54 pp. **ML284.8.D7S7 1978**

Stobbe, Ursula. "Bibliographie der Sächsischen Landesbibliothek 1956–1965." In *Aus der Arbeit der Sächsischen Landesbibliothek 1956–1965,* edited by Burghard Burgemeister, pp. 105–48. Dresden: Sächsische Landesbibliothek, 1966. **Z802.D77 A9**

Streich, Brigitte. *Zwischen Reiseherrschaft und Residenzbildung: Der Wettinische Hof im späten Mittelalter.* Cologne: Böhlau, 1989. xii + 666 pp., ill. **DD801.S37 S77 1989**

Wehler, Hans-Ulrich, ed. *Deutscher Bauernkrieg 1524–1526.* Göttingen: Vandenhoeck & Ruprecht, 1975. 356 pp. **DD182.D48**

Wernaer, Robert Maximilian. *Romanticism and the Romantic School in Germany.* New York: Appleton, 1910. xv + 375 pp. **PT361.W5**

Willoughby, Leonard Ashley. *The Romantic Movement in Germany.* New York: Russell & Russell, 1966. vi + 192 pp. **PT361.W6 1966**

Woody, Thomas. *Fürstenschulen in Germany after t he Reformation.* Menasha, Wis.: George Banta Publishing, 1920. 46 pp., frontispiece, portrait, facs. **LA721.4.W6**

Zeeden, Ernst Walter. *Die Entstehung der Konfessionen.* Munich: Oldenbourg, 1965. 213 pp. **BR305.2.Z4**

Ziolkowski, Theodore. *German Romanticism and Its Institutions.* Princeton: Princeton University Press, 1990. 440 pp. **PT361.Z48 1990**

Zur Mühlen, Karl-Heinz. *Reformatorisches Profil: Studien zum Weg Martin Luthers und der Reformation.* Göttingen: Vandenhoeck & Ruprecht, 1995.

Illustrations

1. *Item 2*

Machsor mechol haschana. (Jewish Holy Day Prayer Book for the Whole Year.) Germany, c. 1290. Vellum.

Moses receives the Ten Commandments and presents them to the people.

This magnificent manuscript is a testimony to German Jewry of the Middle Ages. *Machsorim* (cycles) are the special prayer books for Sabbath and other holy days. The Dresden manuscript contains prayers for the Feast of Weeks, Passover, and the feast commemorating the deliverance of the Jews from a Persian plot, along with poetry by Rabbi Meir von Rothenburg (1215–93) and the renowned Hebrew poet Juda Halevi (1075–1141). Part 2 of this work, containing prayers for the remaining holy days, is located in Wrocław, Poland. Both parts were written by Reuben, a pupil of Rabbi Meir, probably in Esslingen. The beautiful miniatures by an anonymous Gentile illuminator are painted in Christian Gothic style.

2. *Item 6*

Petrarca, Francesco: Des remedes de l'une et l'autre fortune. (Of Remedies for Fortune Fair and Foul.) France, mid-fifteenth century. Vellum.

Scholar and disciple at home.

In 1365 the renowned Italian poet Francesco Petrarca (1304–74) wrote *Of Remedies for Fortune Fair and Foul,* in which he offers advice, in the form of dialogues between Reason and Agony, on thinking clearly in times of happiness and sorrow. The Dresden manuscript, containing Jean Daudin's translation, is dedicated to King Charles VII and is an outstanding example of Flemish fifteenth-century workmanship, with its delicate gold initials and arabesques. Especially outstanding are the two miniatures, the early work of Jacques de Besançon. Before it was acquired for the Dresden collection in 1725, the manuscript had several illustrious French owners: Jacques d'Armagnac, count of Nemours (d. 1477), Antoine de Bourgogne (d. 1564), and Countess Anne Henriette de Condé (d. 1723).

3. *Item 8*

Boccaccio, Giovanni: Des cas des nobles hommes et femmes. (Of the Fate of Illustrious Men and Women.) France, c. 1520. Vol. 2. Vellum.

Boccaccio and his audience.

Though he is today better known for his *Decameron,* until the middle of the sixteenth century Giovanni Boccaccio was most famous for his work *Of the Fate of Illustrious Men and Women.* Using biblical, classical, and mythological examples, he shows how a change in fortune can destroy even the powerful. Written around 1360, this work was soon translated into all the major European languages. Volumes 2–5 of the magnificent manuscript date from 1520 and show that handwritten manuscripts were produced for the wealthy and powerful even after the invention of printing. The dedicatory inscription indicates that Charles de Bourbon gave the volumes to King Francis I of France. Two hundred years later, they were presented to the Saxon elector Augustus the Strong by Prince Karol Stanisław Radziwiłł.

FRANCHINI GAFORI LAVDENSIS . MVSICE ACTIONIS. ¶ LIBER PRIMVS.

¶ De Introductorio ad Muſicam exercitationem neceſſario.

¶ Caput primum.

ET ſi harmonicam ſcientiam plerique ceſſante vſu (quod theorici eſt) lõge auctius quam q̃ ipſa ſunt exercitatione proſequuti : hos tamen ad tantum harmoniæ vſum nulla creditur ſcientia puenire non potuiſſe: Quid enim præſtantiſſimos veteres illos primo theoricæ conſcriptos commemorem: qum Orpheum : Amphionem : Linum thebeum : Arionem & Thimoteum ac reliquos ipſa poſteritas celebrarit : quorum cõcentu (vſu inquam) alter feras : ſaxa alter & ſiluas : Aquatiles beluas alter : agreſteſq; animos & rudes demulxere . hos & diſciplinæ ipſius inſtitutis & ipſa actione cõſtat celeberrimos extitiſſe. Nec temere Pythagoricos ipſos & Platonicos atq; Parhypateticos in medium adduxero : quorum iuſſu diſciplinandis adoleſcentibus & naturalis & artificioſæ vocis vſus plurimum cõmendatur: quod ea quidem ratione aſſertum eſt : quum Ariſtoxenus muſicus atq; Philoſophus teſte Marcho Tullio primo tuſculanarum queſtionum: ipſius corporis intenſionem quãdam velut in cantu & fidibus: quæ harmonia dicitur: ſic ex totius corporis natura & figura varios modos fieri tanq̃ in cãtu ſonos affirmauerit. ¶ Sunt & qui vanas poſuere potentias niſi redigantur ad actus : quare exercitationem melodicæ vocis ſentiunt harmonicæ conſyderationi plurimum contuliſſe: non q; variam ei multitudinem ſed ipſam adhibeat perfectionem. ¶ Eſt igitur muſicæ actio motus ſonorum cõſonantias ac melodiam efficiens . Quos quidem ſonos fruſtra ratione & ſcientia colligimus : niſi ipſa fuerint exercitatione compræhenſi . Hinc eorum Intenſiones remiſſioneſq; ac conſonantias non animo tantum atq; ratione: ſed auditus & pronũtiationis conſuetudine pernoteſcere neceſſe eſt. ¶ Sed neq;

a i

4. *Item 12*
Gaffurius (Gafori), Franchinus: Practica Musicae. (The Performance of Music.) Milan, 1496. Printed on vellum.

Choir and musical cherubs.
From 1451 to 1522 Franchinus Gaffurius, the highly educated conductor of Milan Cathedral, was considered the authority on musical theory. During his lifetime his textbook *Practica Musicae* was published in six editions. He greatly influenced music theory by relating theory and practice and by enhancing the application of intervals and musical notation. The second and fourth editions (Brescia, 1497 and 1508) became items 4 and 5 in the newly established Music Department of the library. Today they are rarer than the first edition. A fine copy of the first edition was purchased by then librarian Falkenstein, who commented on its connection with the library: "Francesco Morlacchi, the last conductor of the Italian Opera House in Dresden, sold this copy to the Königliche Bibliothek in September 1841 shortly before departing for Italy to cure his consumption. He was not to reach his goal: he died October 28 in Innsbruck."

Et sumpturus item. nihil vt mutabile ferret
Humano ponens mortalem tegmine carnem.
post mortem propria cum maiestate refulgens.
Nec sine diuino constat moderamine gestum
Qd vinum cum felle datum. tristemq; saporem
Suscipiens tetigit labijs. & ab ore remouit.
Quippe necem paruo degustaturus amaram
Tempore. quam reduci contemnere carne pararet.
Heu falx torua patrum segetem casura nepotum.
Heu facinus Pylate tuum. quot gesseris vno
Crimina iudicio vigili si mente notares
Nec solas lauisse manus. sed corpore toto
Debueras sacrum veniæ sperare lauacrum.
Corripis insontem. sistis sub præsule regem
Præponisq; humana deo. qua morte teneris.
Qui dominum numerosa cruci per vulnera mittis?

CHRISTVS CRVCIFIXVS.

Hierony ℂ Postq ad caluariæ venit gens impia collem
In terram statuere crucem. cruce deinde supinum
Constituunt Iesum. sanctas quoq; cuspide ferri
Inde manus. atq; inde pedes fixere beatos.
O dolor. o pietas. medium statuere nefandos
Inter latrones. atq; est numeratus in illis.

Baptista. Vt patrias sordes crimenq; aboleret Iesus
Legit inauditum hoc fati genus. illita fuso
Sanguine. & ardenti liuentia verbera membra
Perfossumq; caput. terebrataq; tempora duris
Sentibus. erexit miles romanus in altum
Aera. frigentes plantas. proiectaq; longe
Brachia. & humentes oculos. & pectus apertum

5. *Item 15*
Dürer, Albrecht: Passio Domini Nostri Jesu. (The Passion of Our Lord Jesus.) Nuremberg, 1511.

Christ on the Cross.
The artistic legacy of Albrecht Dürer (1471–1528) includes not only his work as a painter, graphic artist, and draftsman, but also his work as an art historian. This sketchbook contains the master's original drawings and his autograph manuscript of book 1 of his *Proportionslehre* (Guidelines for Proportions). This treasure contains three woodcut series: the life of the Virgin Mary, the Passion of Jesus Christ, and the Apocalypse. Created over a period of time (the leaf on display, for example, dates between 1496 and 1499), they were first gathered in one volume and printed with the Latin verses of Benedict Chelidonius in 1511. The Dresden exemplar owes its special charm to the colorful floral border and its illumination probably done in Dürer's workshop.

80

Neydelhart dacht sol Er von hyn
Also komen zů der Künigin
Mit dem leben frisch vnnd gesund
So wirt zů derselbigen stund
Vnnser gewalt von vnns genomen
Wir möchten auch in leyd komen
Dann Er ist ein ernstlicher Man
Darumb wil Ich weyter fahen an

364

6. *Item 16*

Pfinzing, Melchior: Theuerdank. Augsburg, 1519.

Theuerdank's horse being hit by a bullet.

Emperor Maximilian I (1459–1519) created a literary monument to himself with his poem *Theuerdank,* the only one of several planned literary works to be completed and published during his lifetime. No other book of the time compares with it in typographic and artistic workmanship. Conceived by the emperor himself and written with the assistance of the court poet, Melchior Pfinzing, this allegorical poem in the tradition of the heroic epics describes the young Maximilian's courtship of Maria, heiress to Burgundy. It is one of the earliest books written in *Fraktur* and is enhanced by woodcuts by the artists Hans Burgkmair, Hans Schäufelein, and Leonhard Beck, depicting everyday life at the beginning of the sixteenth century.

7. *Item 19*
Wahrhaftige Abcontrafactur und Bildnis aller Großherzogen von Sachsen. (Authentic Representations and Portraiture of All the Grand Dukes of Saxony.) Dresden, 1586. Vellum.

Elector Friedrich the Wise.
The study of Martin Luther and the Reformation also involves considering the role of Elector Friedrich the Wise (1463–1525). He was a man of profound religious beliefs and broad education with extensive interests in theology, history, and jurisprudence. His court was a vital center of humanistic studies, the arts, and music. In 1502 he founded the University of Wittenberg, where Luther became a professor in 1512. The elector granted Luther protection while publicly remaining neutral. In 1521 he provided Luther safe-conduct to the imperial Diet in Worms and provided him asylum at Wartburg Castle at the risk of endangering his own state. The elector's politics allowed the Reformation to spread.

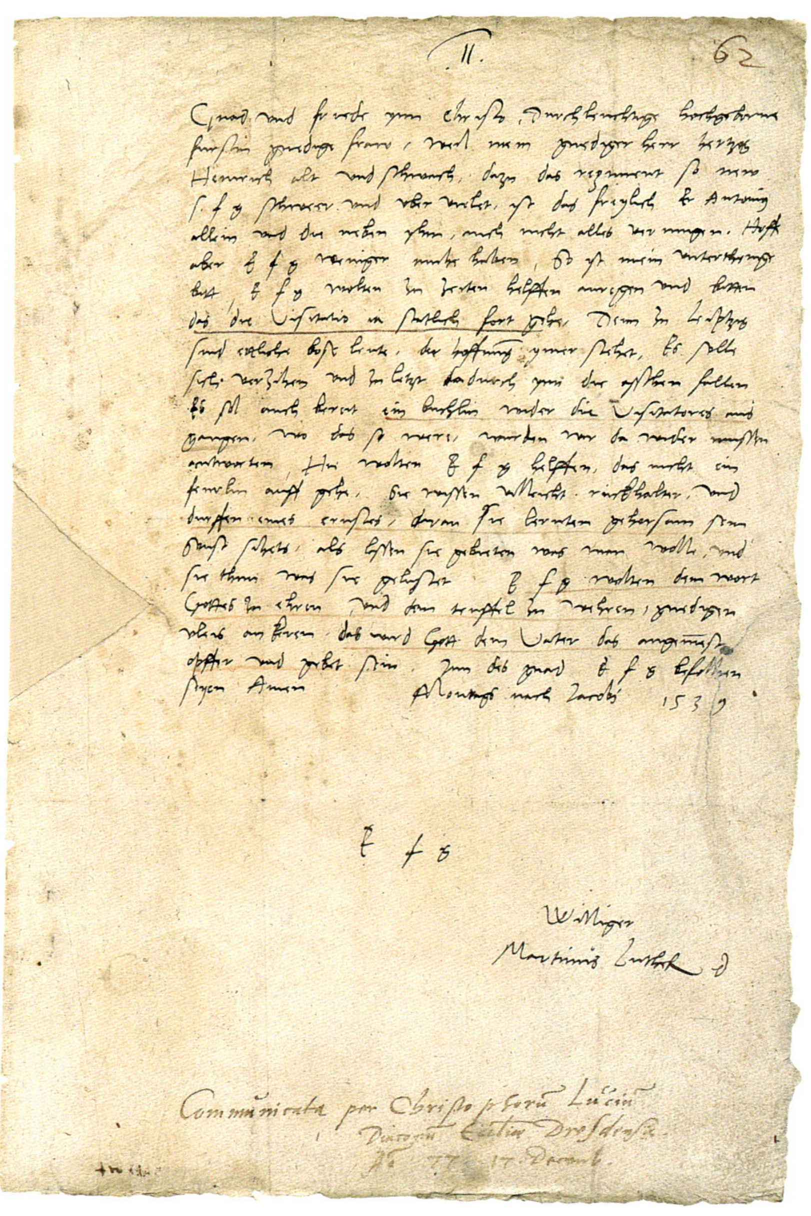

8. *Item 34*

LUTHER, MARTIN: Autograph letter to Duchess Katharina of Saxony. Wittenberg, 28 July 1539.

Duke Georg, ruler of the Albertinian part of Saxony (1471–1539), successfully opposed Luther's Reformation in his state. However, his successor and younger brother, Heinrich (1473–1541), sympathized with the Reformation, supported by his wife Duchess Katharina (1487–1561), who had for years been one of Luther's followers. The Reformation now proceeded in the duchy of Saxony, though with resistance in Leipzig on the part of monks, university theologians, and some members of the city council. Luther's letter of 28 July 1539, opening with the words, "... because my esteemed Lord Duke Heinrich [is] old and frail ...," sought Katharina's support for the implementation of the Reformation in the duchy.

9. *Item 43*
Biblia. (The Bible.) Venice, 1479. Printed on vellum.

The creation of man, the Fall, and the expulsion from Paradise.

Venice's reputation as an early printing center was above all based on the works of Nikolaus Jenson, who from 1470 until his death in 1480 printed ninety-eight known works, primarily classical works and legal and theological literature. His Antiqua type, which recreates the letter forms of Roman inscriptions in modern print, is considered the perfect embodiment of humanistic ideals. This vellum printing of a 1479 Bible is an outstanding incunabulum. In the Dresden exemplar the major initials are illuminated, with the smaller ones in red and blue. The two leaves with miniatures are precious, especially that showing several themes from Genesis.

Gottes wort
bleibt ewig
Biblia/das ist/die
gantze Heilige Sch=
rifft Deudsch.
Mart. Luth.
Wittemberg.
Begnadet mit Kür=
furstlicher zu Sachsen
freiheit.
Gedruckt durch Hans Lufft.
M. D. XXXIIII.

10. *Item 48*

Biblia deutsch. Übersetzt von Martin Luther. (The Bible in German. Translated by Martin Luther.) Wittenberg, 1534.

Title page of the first complete Bible in Luther's translation.

This Bible is considered one of Martin Luther's (1483–1546) greatest linguistic accomplishments. He first translated the New Testament in 1522. His translation of the Old Testament was interrupted by political upheaval and was published in parts until 1534. Luther united the separate sections into a complete Bible and thoroughly revised the text with the assistance of the Wittenberg scholars Philipp Melanchthon, Justus Jonas, and Caspar Cruciger. The work was richly illustrated with historiated initials and 117 woodcuts from the workshop of Lucas Cranach and shows Luther's strong influence on its pictorial themes. It was completed in September 1534 and sold at the Leipzig fair that October for 2 guilders, 8 groschen for an unbound copy. For comparison, a schoolmaster of the time earned approximately 4 guilders annually.

11. *Item 52*
Biblia Germanico-Latina. (German-Latin Bible.) Wittenberg, 1565. Printed on vellum.

Saxon elector Augustus.
In numerous manuscripts and books is the statement that they were written or printed "by order of" Elector Augustus (1526–86). Thus, in 1565 he had printed in Wittenberg at his expense this twenty-volume Bible in Latin and German, partly on vellum, and richly decorated with colored miniatures and initials. In each volume is an illuminated woodcut portrait of the elector after a painting by Lucas Cranach the Younger. Several sets, beautifully bound, were given to friendly princes. Displayed here is the private copy of Elector Augustus, which includes a unique vellum sheet with the inscription: "His lordship the elector of Saxony began reading this Bible on June 9 in the year [15]85 and finished on August 23 of the same year. It took ten weeks and five days."

12. *Item 57*
KENTMANN, JOHANNES: Kräuterbuch.
(Book of Herbs.) 1563.

Red apples from the New World (tomato plants). Johannes Kentmann (1518–74) was the typical sixteenth-century German scientist. Born in Dresden, he studied in Leipzig and Wittenberg, and in Bologna, Italy, where he earned his doctorate in medicine and surgery. In his long career as a principal physician at Torgau, he wrote on many scientific subjects. In 1563, commissioned by Elector August, he compiled his *Kräuterbuch* (Book of Herbs), a systematic arrangement of approximately 600 illustrations of trees, bushes, shrubs, and domestic and wild plants, executed by the Torgau artist, David Redtel. The *Kräuterbuch* was never printed, and this unique manuscript remains a treasure of the Saxon State Library.

61.

13. *Item 60*
Mair, Paulus Hector: Fecht-, Ring- und Turnierbuch. (Book of Fencing, Wrestling, and Jousting.) Mid-sixteenth century.

Duel with long swords.
In the Middle Ages fencing and wrestling were not only exercises for war preparation but also a favorite art form at social events for the nobility and the city society. Fencing and wrestling champions traveled from town to town participating in exhibition bouts and giving lessons. Books on these subjects were popular, particularly in the sixteenth century. Even Albrecht Dürer wrote a work on fencing. This manuscript by Paulus Hector Mair (1517–79) contains 242 vivid illustrations depicting duels with swords, with halberds, and even with toothed sickles. The author died a tragic death: after forty-four years in service to the city of Augsburg, he was hanged for misappropriation of public funds.

62.

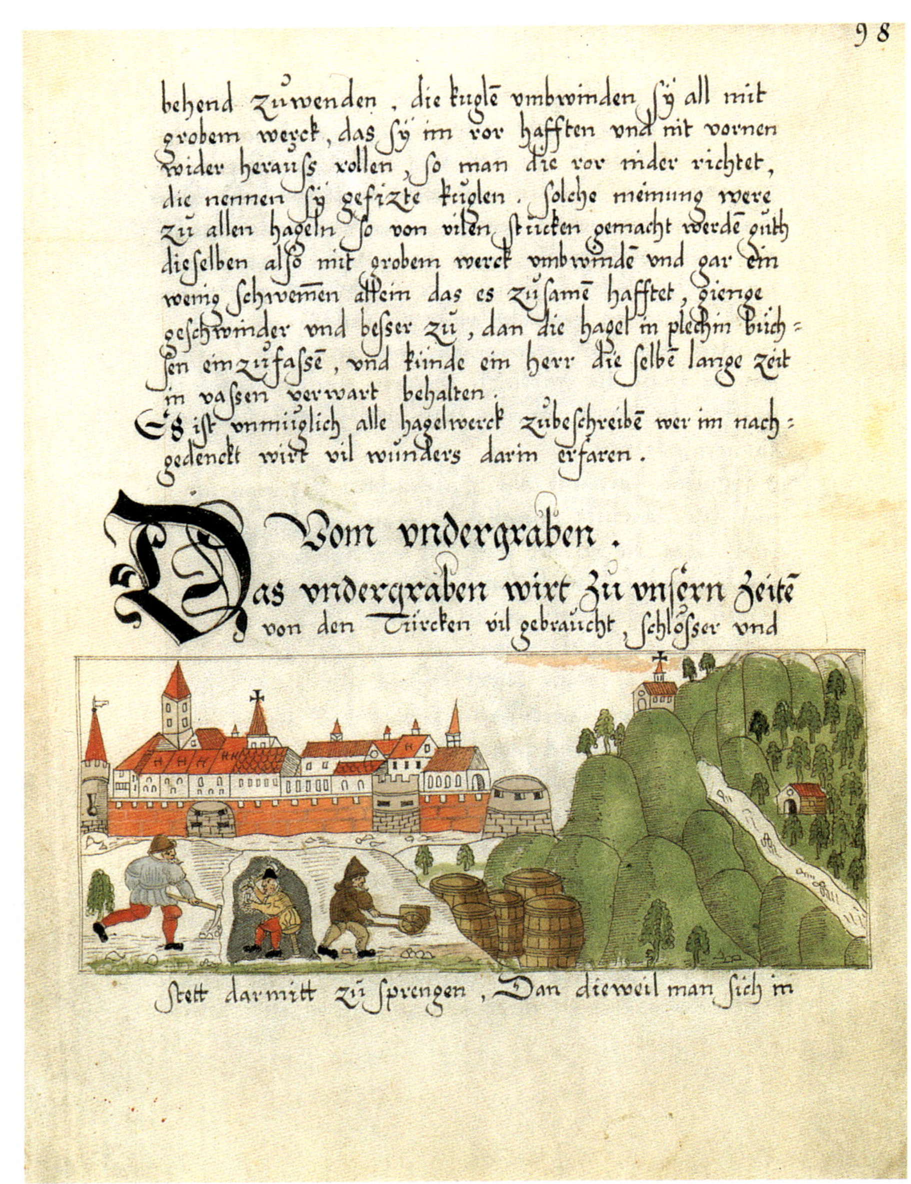

98

behend zuwenden, die kuglē umbwinden sy all mit
grobem werck, das sy im vor hafften und mit vornen
wider herauss vollen, so man die vor nider richtet,
die nennen sy gefizte kuglen. Solche meinung were
zu allen hageln so von vilen stucken gemacht werdē unth
dieselben also mit grobem werck umbwindē und gar ein
wenig schwemen allein das es zusamē hafftet, gienge
geschwinder und besser zu, dan die hagel in plechin buch-
sen einzufassē, und kunde ein herr dieselbē lange zeit
in vassen verwart behalten.
Es ist unmuglich alle hagelwerck zubeschreibē wer im nach-
gedenckt wirt vil wunders darin erfaren.

Vom undergraben.

Das undergraben wirt zu unsern zeitē
von den Turcken vil gebraucht, schlosser und
stett darmitt zu sprengen, Dan dieweil man sich in

14. *Item 61*

Senftenberg, Veit Wolff von: Kriegserfindungen. (Military Inventions.) Second half of sixteenth century.

Mining of a fortress.

Military historians consider Veit Wolff von Senftenberg a leading authority on artillery of his day. Around 1570 he wrote *Kriegserfindungen (Military Inventions),* based on his own experience and designed to help defeat the Turks, from whose attacks Senftenberg himself had suffered. To assure secrecy he did not allow the work to be printed. This Dresden copy, a parchment manuscript with informative, colorful pictures, describes the different weapons and their most effective use. In fighting the Turks, poisoning the water supply was considered permissible and an effective and secure communication network was essential.

15. *Item 62*
Loeneyss, Georg Engelhart: Gründlicher Bericht und Ordnung der Gebisse. (Thorough Report on Equestrian Dentistry.) 1576.

A young stallion and the bit.
This manuscript, magnificently bound by Jakob Krause, belonged to Elector August's private library. The author was from 1523 to 1584 both the elector's equerry and the person responsible for arranging all official court functions. His *Della cavalleria,* continually reprinted into the eighteenth century, was the summation of his experience in these fields. The Dresden manuscript depicts not only the numerous horse bits, reins, muzzles, and grooming implements, but also the horses themselves, outfitted with saddles, ornamental harnesses, and blankets, and a complete tournament.

XX.

Die Statt Secota.

Es seind die Stätte/ so mit keinen Pfälen vmbringet/ gemeiniglichen lustiger als die andern/ wie diese Figur/ so die Statt Secota genennet wirdt/ rechte contrafactur außweiset. Dann daselbst sind hin vnd her Häuser vnnd Gärten/ wie der Buchstab E. bezeichnet/ in welchen wächst das Tabaco/ von jhnen Vppowoc genennet. Es sind auch vmb dieselben Wälde/ in welchen sie Hirsche fangen. So seind auch daselbst Ecker/ darinn sie jhr Korn sähen. Auff den Eckern bawen sie ein gerüst/ vnd darauff ein Häußlein oder Hütten/ welches sie nach art eines halben Circkels bedecken/ wie der Buchstab F. bedeutet. In diesem bestellen sie ein Wechter/ dann es seind allda so viel Vögel vnnd Thier/ daß/ so fern sie nicht fleissig wacheten/ der Samen in kurtzer zeit auffgefressen würde/ dessen wegen muß der Wechter ohn vnterlaß ruffen/ vnd ein geresch machen. Den Samen aber sähē sie auff eine solche ordnung/ welchs der Buchstab H. außweiset/ sonst würde das eine gewächß durch das ander erstickt/ vnd das Korn/ wie sichs gebürt/ nicht reiff werden/ dann seine Bletter sind so groß als die Bletter deß grossen Rors/ wie am Buchstaben G. zu sehen. Sie haben auch einen sonderlichen Platz/ mit C. gezeichnet/ auff welchem/ wann sie mit jhren Nachbawren alldā zusammen kommen/ jhre järliche hohe Fest (davan in der achtzehenden Figuren geredt jst worden) begehen. Darnach gehen sie auff einen ort/ durch den Buchstaben D. bedeutet/ vnd halten daselbst jre Gastereyen. Gegen vber haben sie einen runden Boden/ mit dem Buchstaben B. gezeichnet/ dahin sie sich/ jhr Jarzeitliches Gebett zu thun/ versamlen. Nicht ferrn von diesem ist ein weites Gebäw/ mit A. gezeichnet/ in welchem der grosser Hërrn Begräbnusse sind/ wie auß der zwey vnd zwantzigsten Figuren erscheinen wirdt. Sie habē auch Gärten/ in welchen sie eine Frucht/ einem Apffel oder Pfeben gleichförmig/ ziehen/ durch den Buchstaben J. bezeichnet. So haben sie gleicher weise einen ort/ durch K. angedeutet/ auff welchem sie zu zeiten jrer hohen Feste ein Fewer anzünden. Draussen/ nicht ferrn von der Statt/ haben sie ein fliessendes Wasser/ durch L. angedeutet/ auß welchem sie Wasser schöpffen. Es machen sich derwegen diese Leut/ mit gar keinem Geitz beladen/ lustig vnd frölich. Vnd nach dem sie jhre grosse Fest bey Nacht begehen vnnd halten/ dero wegen legen sie helle vnd liechte Fewer an/ zum ersten darumb/ daß sie nicht im finstern strauchlen/ zum andern/ daß sie jhre frewde vnter einander zu verstehen geben.

16. *Item 67*
Harriot, Thomas: Customs of the Savages in Virginia. Frankfurt am Main, 1590.

Indian settlement.
Thomas Harriot (1560–1621) was official surveyor for the expedition led by Sir Richard Grenville in 1585–86 to Roanoke Island off the coast of present-day North Carolina. This German edition, published in Frankfurt by Theodor de Bry in 1590, two years after the first edition appeared in London, was dedicated by the publisher to Saxon elector Christian I (1560–91). Harriot presents a vivid picture of the conditions he observed in this part of the New World, especially the natural resources and their possible use by English settlers, as well as the habits and customs of the native inhabitants. The twenty-three full-page engravings, after originals by the Dutch artist Johann With, and hand colored in the Dresden exemplar, add to the value of this work.

17. *Item 68*
Bretschneider, Daniel: Ein Buch von allerlei Inventionen zu Schlittenfahrten. (A Book of Various Inventions for Sled Travel.) Dresden, 1602.

Sled with astronomer.
In 1602 the Dresden painter Daniel Bretschneider presented Elector Christian II with several designs for sleds. He was awarded 50 guilders for his efforts. Emulating the great courts of France, Italy, England, and Spain, the Saxon rulers used sleds of the best design in opulent pageants. Birthdays, weddings, baptisms, and carnivals were occasions to stage such events, which often had biblical, mythological, and exotic themes, as well as everyday motifs celebrating the trades of Saxony, such as the mining industry. These pageants played an important role in enhancing the ruler's image before his subjects and other rulers. This custom is well documented, in part by the survival of so many Saxon illustrated manuscripts of the sixteenth–eighteenth centuries.

18. *Item 69*
Tierhatz auf dem Altmarkt zu Dresden. (Animal Chase in Dresden's Altmarkt.) 1609.

The boar chase.
The event documented in this illustrated manuscript appears bizarre to us today. Eight large leaves depict the Altmarkt in Dresden at carnival time, entirely surrounded by buildings, with the City Hall (Rathaus) to the north. Animals, including deer, boar, bears, wolves, rabbits, wildcats, foxes and raccoons, were brought in, chased, and killed before hundreds of spectators. The show, in this case a boar hunt, culminated in a battle between bears and bulls. Such public chases offered city dwellers the opportunity to experience the thrill of the hunt enjoyed for centuries by the court.

67.

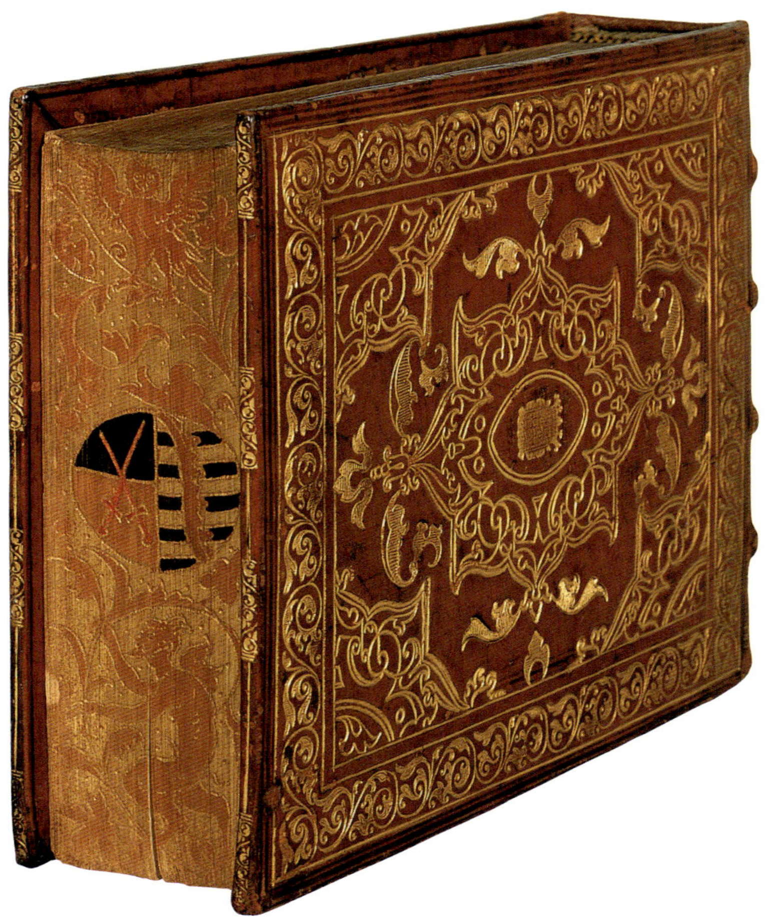

19. *Item 70*
Division Tables. c. 1570. Binding by Jakob Krause, with electoral coat of arms.

Shortly after Elector August began collecting books, he hired Jakob Krause, one of the best Renaissance bookbinders. Krause (1526/27–85) was born in Zwickau. After completing his bookbinding apprenticeship, he improved his skills in Wittenberg and in France. He served for several years as a binder to the renowned merchant house of Fugger in Augsburg. In 1566 he came to Dresden, where he eventually produced more than a thousand magnificent bindings. In addition, he purchased books for the elector, visiting the trade fairs in Frankfurt and Leipzig. Krause's bindings are distinguished by meticulous workmanship and rich decoration. They exemplify German bookbinding style as practiced in Wittenberg, but incorporating French, Italian, and oriental motifs, which Krause merged with his own style. This example shows his skill in ornamentation and chasing.

20. *Item 71*
Paul, Simon: Postilla. Magdeburg, 1572. Binding by Urban Köblitz.

With the richly ornamental and colorful binding of this volume, Urban Köblitz demonstrates that he was among the outstanding bookbinders in Saxony, along with Jakob Krause and Caspar Meuser (see figures 19 and 21). All that is known of him is that he worked in Dresden and later in Leipzig.

21. *Item 74*
Betbüchlein für allerlei Anliegen. (Small Prayer Book for All Occasions.) c. 1580. Heart-shaped binding by Caspar Meuser.

Caspar Meuser (1550–93) was an apprentice of Jakob Krause and, from 1574, Krause's successor in the court bindery. He used the panels and stamps designed by Krause, but evolved his own style, characterized by profuse vinework. This heart-shaped prayerbook, designed for Anna, the wife of Elector August, is a particularly fine example of his artistry.

22. *Item 80*

Bretschneider, Daniel: Contrafactur des Ringrennens und anderer Ritterspiele auf Christians fürstlichem Beilager am 25. April Anno [15]82 in Dresden. (Contrafactum of the Ring Competition and Other Knightly Games at the Princely Consummation of Christian's Marriage on April 25 of the Year [15]82 in Dresden.) Dresden, c. 1582.

Procession with members of the Hofkapelle dressed as women.

The Dresden court had a long and splendid tradition of designing fancy-dress festivals in the city. Members of the Hofkapelle not only performed as musicians in the festival processions, but also dressed in lavish costumes as actors. The item on display, originally a scroll and later bound in book form, describes the ceremonies on the occasion of an electoral wedding. Elector August is preceded here by enchained figures representing Death, the Devil, Justice, two Heralds, and the Muses. Members of the Hofkapelle with their instruments can be identified in the procession. The instruments were described a generation later by Michael Praetorius in his *Syntagma musicum.*

23. *Item 89*
Collection of Portraits of the Counts of Saxony. Seventeenth century.

Elector Johann Georg I.
This portrait of the elector is one in a series of fifty-two impressive miniatures on vellum depicting Saxony's rulers from the sixteenth century on. Johann Georg I commissioned the miniatures, which took as their models the late sixteenth-century life-size portraits hanging at court. Later miniatures carried the series to the end of the seventeenth century in the representation of August the Strong, Saxon elector and king of Poland. The long rule (1611–56) of Elector Johann Georg I (1585–1656), dominated by the Thirty Years' War, brought to an end Saxony's role as a power in Europe.

24. *Item 103*

Biblia. Übersetzt von Martin Luther. (The Bible. Translated by Martin Luther.) Nuremberg, 1652.

Bible of Elector Moritz of Sachsen-Zeitz, with his coat of arms.

The velvet-bound Bible on display is an example of the book treasures that came to the Dresden Court Library. The head of the Albertinian line, Elector Johann Georg I, proclaimed that upon his death Saxony should be divided among his four sons. His youngest son, Moritz (1619–81), became the ruler of the new duchy of Sachsen-Zeitz. Although this may have been a politically dubious decision, the duchy benefited culturally. The new duke's dynamic building program soon remedied the destruction caused by the Thirty Years' War. Moritz Castle (Moritzburg) in Zeitz was an early example of baroque architecture. The duke also supported the arts and music.

25. *Item 108*
Atlas Royal. Vol. 1. Amsterdam, 1707.

Queen Anne of England.
This unique atlas testifies to both the love of splendor and the interest in science of August the Strong (1670–1733). The atlas was produced for him in Amsterdam, once the center of the map trade, in 1706–10. In nineteen large-format morocco volumes, the atlas contains roughly 1,400 beautifully illuminated, printed or hand-drawn leaves (maps, views, plans, portraits), primarily of Dutch and French—less often of Italian, English, or German—origin dating to the seventeenth and early eighteenth centuries. The volume on display contains fifty priceless, masterfully tinted engravings, depicting English court dress around 1700.

26. *Item 109*
Pöppelmann, Matthäus Daniel: Entwurf für einen Zwingerpavillon. (Draft for a Zwinger pavilion.) Dresden, 1712–13.

The Dresden Zwinger, a masterpiece of baroque architecture, would have been inconceivable without the initiative and influence of August the Strong. Two of the foremost artists of the era, the architect Matthäus Daniel Pöppelmann (1662–1736) and the sculptor Balthasar Permoser (1651–1732), executed his concept. Initially, the project was to involve merely the construction of an orangery in the Zwinger section of the fortress complex. But the plans grew more elaborate in conjunction with the proposed construction of a new castle. Original plans in the Saxon State Library show the grand scale of the overall concept, of which only the Zwinger was realized, in modified form. The rampart shown here as a rectangular structure, for example, was ultimately built in a more graceful oval form.

27. *Item 117*

Bach, Johann Sebastian: Missa (h moll: Kyrie und Gloria). Originaler Stimmensatz. (Mass in B Minor: Kyrie and Gloria. Original Vocal Part.) Leipzig, 1733.

Manuscript score.

From his arrival in Dresden in 1717, Bach maintained lifelong contact with the court and the Hofkapelle, where the highest musical standards found expression. After the death of Hofkapellmeister Heinichen in 1729 and the appointment of J. A. Hasse as his replacement, Bach (who was not considered for the position for religious reasons) applied for a court appointment. To his application he appended a part of his *Mass in B Minor.* Pressed for time, Bach enlisted his wife and eldest son in transcribing the work. The date of the first Dresden performance of this brilliant work has never been determined. However, since 1736 the cantor of the St. Thomas Church in Leipzig has carried the title of "composer to the court of the king of Poland and the elector of Saxony."

28. *Item 123*
Merian, Maria Sibylla: Metamorphosis insectorum Surinamensium. (Metamorphosis of the Insects of Surinam.) Amsterdam, 1705.

Jasmine bush with butterfly and snake.
In 1699 a woman set out on a journey. Her destination was unusual and her purpose even more so: Maria Sibylla Merian (1647–1717) journeyed from Holland to Surinam to study and depict insects. The results of her two-year stay in the jungle were published in 1705 in a large-format folio, which earned her a place of honor among naturalists. Trained as a painter and obsessed with a desire for knowledge, she studied and drew the insects in their various developmental stages and the plants she found them on. The Saxon State Library is fortunate to own one of the few surviving copies of Merian's work, one colored by the author-artist herself.

29. *Item 138*
Plans et élévations des différentes églises. (Plans and Elevations of Various Churches.) First half of eighteenth century.

Original cross-sectional drawing of the Frauenkirche by Georg Bähr.
Known as the Stone Bell, the dome of the Frauenkirche rose above the inner city of Dresden for more than two centuries until it collapsed during the bombing at the end of World War II. A serious commitment has recently been made to rebuild this most important example of Protestant church architecture, giving hope that the cherished landmark will once again dominate Dresden's skyline by the city's eight-hundredth anniversary in 2006. The church is the work of Georg Bähr (1666–1738), one of the great German baroque builders, noted for his unique style in Protestant architecture. In keeping with the special features of Protestant worship, he created a central structure in which the altar, pulpit, baptismal font, and organ were all located in full view of the congregation beneath the bell-shaped stone dome. Shown here is the original drawing with handwritten approval (dated 26 June 1726) by Count August Christoph von Wackerbarth, superintendent of Saxon architecture. Construction was begun two months later. The church was dedicated in 1734, but the last stone was not laid until 1743.

30. *Item 139*

WAGNER, RICHARD: Das Liebesmahl der Apostel. Biblische Szene für Männerstimmen und großes Orchester. (The Love Feast of the Apostles. Biblical Scene for Male Voices and Large Orchestra.) Autograph Score. Dresden, 1843.

Richard Wagner, Hofkapellmeister in Dresden from 1842 until his flight in 1849, wrote this unique work as a "stereophonic" dialogue among several choir groups, followed by the entrance of full orchestra. It had its premiere under his direction at the Dresden Frauenkirche on 6 July 1843. Twelve hundred Saxon singers are said to have participated in the choirs, and the premiere was an extraordinary success.

79.

31. *Item 141*
Reinhold, Friedrich Johann Christian: Uniformen der kurfürstlich sächsischen Armee. (Uniforms of the Army of the Electorate of Saxony.) 1791.

City commander and adjutant on the Neumarkt. Dresden, the capital of Albertinian Saxony since 1485, was expanded into a fortress in the sixteenth century. It was protected by the citizenry until 1587, when a regular garrison was established. Elector Johann Georg III (1647–91) created a standing army in 1682, and the office of commandant was created for Dresden in 1692. One of the duties of the commandant and his adjutants was opening and closing three city gates and lowering and raising the drawbridges. The illustration shows the commandant and adjutant, oversized, in colorful uniform, in the Dresden Neumarkt, with the Frauenkirche and the Art Gallery to the left.

32. *Item 143*
Dresden. View of the City from the Southwest. End of eighteenth century.

At the beginning of the nineteenth century, the Dresden painter Christian Gottlieb Hammer (1779–1864) depicted his city from a particularly attractive perspective. From the confluence of the Weisseritz and Elbe Rivers, he had a view of both parts of the city: to the left, the Japanese Palace (home of the Dresden Court Library since 1786), the Neustadt (New Town), and the Elbe River bridge (above it the gardens and buildings of the Brühlian terrace and below, the bell tower of the Frauenkirche); to the right, the steeple and nave of the Catholic Hofkirche, the castle tower (the tallest city edifice), and the steeple of the Kreuzkirche in the background.

/: Winckelmann /

Gedancken
über die
Nachahmung der Griechischen
Wercke
in der
Mahlerey und Bildhauer-Kunst.

Vos exemplaria Græca
Nocturna versate manu, versate diurna.
HORAT. ART. POET.

1755.

33. *Item 144*
WINCKELMANN, JOHANN JOACHIM: Gedanken über die Nachahmung der griechischen Werke. (Thoughts on the Imitation of Greek Works.) Friedrichstadt near Dresden, 1755.

Title page.
This was the first publication of Johann Joachim Winckelmann (1717–68), a mere forty-page brochure, of which fifty copies were printed. As a result, the author became famous overnight in the intellectual and artistic world. Winckelmann founded the science of archaeology and the modern study of art with this work and his 1764 Dresden publication, *Geschichte der Kunst des Altertums.* Pivotal to his insights was his study of archaeological literature and of the ancient sculpture in the Dresden art museum—opportunities afforded to him by his seven-year residence in Dresden and his tenure as librarian to Heinrich Count von Bünau.

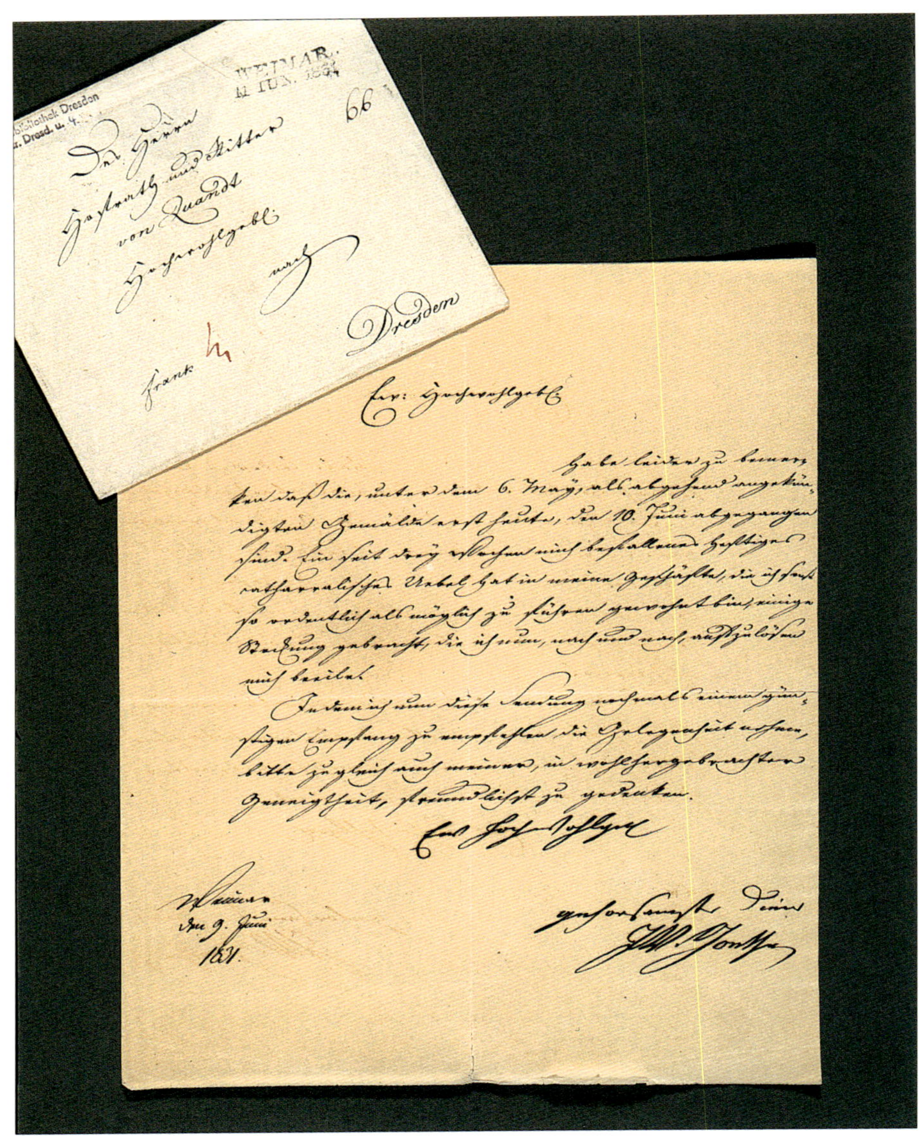

34. *Item 147*
Goethe, Johann Wolfgang von: Letter to Johann Gottlob von Quandt. Weimar, 9 June 1831.

In the course of his life, Johann Wolfgang von Goethe (1749–1832) stayed several times in Dresden. As a student at Leipzig, he visited the city in March 1768, recalling decades later in his *Dichtung und Wahrheit* the deep impression the Art Gallery had made on him. On a journey to Silesia, he visited the Electoral Library on 30 July 1790, as can be seen from his entry in the guest book, which is still in existence. Besides other visits in 1794, 1810, and 1813, Goethe maintained a host of written contacts, officially with the court and privately with the intellectual elite of Dresden. In the letter of 9 June 1831, the poet writes to the renowned art scholar and collector, Johann Gottlob von Quandt (1787–1859), informing him of a shipment of paintings by Weimar artists to Dresden.

35. *Item 159*
Plantae selectae vivis coloribus depictae. (Selected Plants Shown in True-to-Life Colors.) Centuria 1. 1785–95.

Pitcairnia (Bromeliaceae).
The Saxon State Library owns a unique compendium in nine folio volumes, each with roughly one hundred original pictures, of the native and foreign plants raised in the gardens and greenhouses of Pillnitz Castle, the summer residence of the Saxon rulers, around 1800. This extraordinary compilation was proposed and financed by Elector Friedrich August III (1750–1827), who was himself an amateur botanist. Desiring that the plants be depicted faithfully, in a manner both scientifically accurate and artistically appealing, he appointed as "botanical court painters" artists who were already recognized as talented plant painters, finding them among the graduates of his own Dresden Academy of Art. The final volume was completed in 1839, under King Friedrich August II, to the same high standards established in 1785 with volume 1.

36. *Item 174*
Family Album of Johann Gottlieb Schwender. 1795–1810.

View from the Elbe Bridge toward the eastern part of the city.

Family albums *(Stammbücher)* provide remarkable insights into the emotional lives of our ancestors. Known since the sixteenth century and originally popular primarily among the nobility, intellectuals, and students, these books evolved in the late eighteenth and nineteenth centuries into the "monuments to friendship" common in all social classes. Between friends and acquaintances it was common to ask for, and have entered into these books, thoughtful sayings, often in combination with paintings, drawings, and even embroidery, since women also eagerly participated in this custom. The specimen on display, from around 1800, belonged to a Dresden construction official. His friends and acquaintances were in large part architects and artists. For this reason, some of the drawings are of high quality, such as the view from the Elbe Bridge.

37. *Item 176*
Rost, G. E.: Trachten der Berg- und Hüttenleute im Königreich Sachsen. (Traditional Dress of the Mining and Metallurgical Workers in the Kingdom of Saxony.) c. 1830.

Metalworker in work clothes.
Since the Middle Ages, mining had been the major basis for Saxony's wealth, the power of its rulers, and its cultural development. Silver was mined in the Erzgebirge, primarily for coinage, from the twelfth century on. Later tin, copper, iron, coal, cobalt, alum, and small amounts of gold were mined as well. G. E. Rost documented the various aspects of the miner's life, his rich festive dress, his work clothes, his workplace, and his tools, in a book containing plates of considerable significance to students of cultural history.

38. *Item 178*
SCHUMANN, ROBERT: Des Sennen Abschied. (Senn's Farewell.) Lyrics by Friedrich Schiller. No. 22 from "Songs for the Young," Opus 79. Dresden, undated.

Second part of the song in manuscript, first draft. Robert and Clara Schumann lived in Dresden from 1844 to 1850. Robert, however, could not find a permanent position in the city, where he directed a choir. Clara, despite the birth of several children during this period, provided for the family by giving concerts. Nevertheless, the couple found ample intellectual and artistic inspiration, as is shown by the number of important compositions that Robert Schumann created in Dresden. The leaf on display is not only a testimony to Schumann's Dresden creativity but also a historical document. At the bottom of the page the composer noted: "interrupted by the alarm bells on May 3, 1849." On this day there began a revolt of citizens, after the failure of which Richard Wagner, along with the great architect Gottfried Semper and other notable figures, deserted Dresden.

39. *Item 179*
Brahms, Johannes: An ein Veilchen. Text von Ludwig Hölty. Lied für eine Singstimme und Klavier, op. 49,2. (To a Violet. Lyrics by Ludwig Hölty. Song for Voice and Piano, opus 49.2.) Before 1872.

Manuscript, final copy.
On 13 June 1845, soon after the birth of their third daughter on 11 March, Robert and Clara Schumann began an album in Dresden "to our children for faithful safekeeping." It held memorabilia (locks of hair, drawings, dried flowers, poems, compositions, letters) from their closest friends and relatives. Later, particularly after Robert's death, Clara added autograph music by important composers whom she had never met, including a draft leaf by Beethoven. A late addition to the album is the autograph score by Johannes Brahms, who as a youth of twenty was taken into the inner circle of the family and enthusiastically encouraged in composing by Robert. According to Clara's notation in the upper righthand corner of page 1, Brahms presented her the final copy of his 1868 song (Opus 49.2), on ornamental paper, on 13 September 1872, her birthday. It was unsigned, so Clara later added his name as well (at the end of the manuscript, on page 4). In 1934 the Saxon State Library acquired this Dresden album from Schumann's grandsons.

40. *Item 182*
Falnameh. Persia. End of the sixteenth century. Muhammad splits the moon.

In 1831, when Leipzig orientalist Heinrich Fleischer published his catalog of oriental manuscripts in the Royal Public Library, he included a *falnameh,* a Persian book of prophesies. Such books were used to predict the future, for example, the course of a journey or the success of a business deal. It is not known how this precious manuscript came into the possession of the library; a note in it indicates that the manuscript came to Vienna around 1700 during the Turkish wars. The varying styles of painting, artistic quality, format, and design of the text suggest that the manuscript was compiled from leaves of various origin, probably based in part on Persian models in Turkey. It can be dated to the second half of the sixteenth century.

Appendix: Exhibit Checklist

Selected by Manfred Mühlner

Manuscripts from the Medieval-Renaissance

1.
Evangelia dominicalia et festivalia. (Lord's Day and Feast Day Gospels.) Tenth century. 189 leaves. Vellum. 24 x 20 cm.
A: Leaves 59b–60a
Latin Gospel passage used in Catholic Mass.

2. *See figure 1.*
Machsor mechol haschana. (Jewish Holy Day Prayer Book for the Whole Year.) Germany, c. 1290. 293 leaves. Vellum. 55 x 46 cm.
A: Leaves 59b–60a
Moses receives the Ten Commandments.

3.
Bernardus Guidonis: De regibus Francorum. (About the Kings of the Franks.) France, fourteenth century. 30 leaves. Vellum. 28 x 22 cm.
A: Leaves 19b–20a
Genealogy of the French kings from the fifth to the fourteenth century.

4.
Ovid: Metamorphoseon libri XV. (The Fifteen Books of the Metamorphoses.) Italy, fourteenth century. 149 leaves. Vellum. 26 x 16 cm.
A: Leaves 88b–89a
Ovid's metamorphoses.

5.
Romain, Henri: Gestes et faits des anciens. (Acts and Deeds of the Ancients.) France, beginning of fifteenth century. 199 leaves. Vellum. 41 x 29 cm.
A: Leaves 3b–4a
Chronology of the ancient world with a depiction of the building of Rome.

6. *See figure 2.*
Petrarca, Francesco: Des remedes de l'une et l'autre fortune. (Of Remedies for Fortune Fair and Foul.) France, mid-fifteenth century. 206 leaves. Vellum. 41 x 29 cm.
A: Leaves 14b–15a
Francesco Petrarca and a disciple at home.

7.
Annales Veterocellenses, with continuation to the year 1493. (Annals of Altzella.) Germany, end of fifteenth century. 32 leaves. 32.5 x 22.5 cm.
A: Leaves 4b–5a
Manuscript from Altzella, the most important medieval cloister in the margraviate of Meissen.

8. *See figure 3.*
Boccaccio, Giovanni: Des cas des nobles hommes et femmes. (Of the Fate of Illustrious Men and Women.) France, c. 1520. Vol. 2. 94 leaves. Vellum. 51 x 37 cm.
A: Leaves 1b–2a
Boccaccio and his audience.

9.
Kronika Czechu od poczatku yasyku Czeske. (Chronicle of Czechs from the Beginning of the Czech Language.) Bohemia, 1527. 97 leaves. Vellum. 51 x 37 cm.
A: Leaves 92b–93a
The history of Bohemia.

Incunabula: Examples of Early Printing

10.
Horatius Flaccus, Quintus: Opera. (Works.) Florence, 1482. 272 leaves. 29 x 22 cm.
A: Beginning of the first book
Florentine printing of Horace's Works, 1482.

11.
Chroniques de France. (Chronicles of France.) Vol. 3. Paris, 1493. 264 leaves. 35 x 27.5 cm.
A: Leaves 164b–165a
A fifteenth century chronicle of France, by the Benedictine monk Jean Chartier.

12. *See figure 4.*
Gaffurius (Gafori), Franchinus: Practica musicae. (The Performance of Music.) Milan, 1496. 111 leaves. Vellum. 27.5 x 19 cm.
A: Beginning of the first book

13.
Missale Misnense. (Meissen Missal.) Speyer, c. 1498. 238 leaves. Vellum. 38 x 29 cm.
A: Vellum leaf, inserted without numbering
Missal for the Meissen diocese, from the printing shop of Peter Drach.

14.
Danse macabre. (Dance of Death.) Troyes, after 1500. 40 leaves. 26 x 19.5 cm.
A: Leaves a ii–a iii
Old French Dance of Death poem, with colored woodcuts.

The Reformation in Sixteenth Century Germany

15. *See figure 5.*
Dürer, Albrecht: Passio Domini Nostri Jesu. (The Passion of Our Lord Jesus.) Nuremberg, 1511. 46 leaves. 49 x 33 cm.
A: Leaves 24b–25a
The crucifiction by Albrecht Dürer.

16. *See figure 6.*
Pfinzing, Melchior: Theuerdank. Augsburg, 1519. 580 pages. 35 x 26.5 cm.
A: Pages 364–365
Theuerdank, an allegorical poem by Emperor Maximilian I.

17.
Annaberger Chorbuch Nr. 2. Sächsische Musikhandschrift. (Annaberg Choir Book No. 2. Saxon Music Manuscript.) First third of sixteenth century. 261 leaves. 40 x 28 cm.
A: Leaf 112
Example of the musical usage of the Church in central Germany shortly before the Reformation.

18.
Emser, Hieronymus: Divi Bennonis Misnensis quondam Episcopi vita. (The Life of Saint Benno, Former Bishop of Meissen.) Leipzig, 1512. 17 leaves. 30 x 20 cm.
A: Title page
Biography of Bishop Benno of Meissen (d. 1106), Saxony's only saint.

19. *See figure 7.*
Wahrhaftige Abcontrafactur und Bildnis aller Großherzogen von Sachsen. (Authentic Representations and Portraiture of All the Grand Dukes of Saxony.) Dresden, 1586. 44 leaves. Vellum. 21 x 16 cm.
A: Leaf 24a
Portrait of Elector Friedrich the Wise.

20.
Luther, Martin: Von der Freiheit eines Christenmenschen. (On the Freedom of a Christian.) Wittenberg, 1520. 12 leaves. 20 x 15 cm.
A: Title page
The freedom of the new belief.

21.
Luther, Martin: Von dem babylonischen Gefängnis der Kirche. (On the Babylonian Captivity of the Church.) Wittenberg, 1520. 71 leaves. 21 x 15.5 cm.
A: Title page, with portrait of the Reformer
Examination of Roman Catholic sacramental doctrine.

22.
LUTHER, MARTIN: An den christlichen Adel deutscher Nation. Von des christlichen Standes Besserung. (To the Christian Nobility of the German Nation. On the Reformation of the Christian Class.) Wittenberg, 1520. 35 leaves. 21 x 15.5 cm.
A: Title page
Comprehensive program for the reform of the Church.

23.
Passional Christi und Antichristi. (Passion of the Christ and Antichrist.) Wittenberg, 1521. 14 leaves. 20 x 14 cm.
A: Pages 15–16.
Renowned woodcut series by Lucas Cranach the Elder (1472–1553), a friend of Luther.

24.
LUTHER, MARTIN: Ordnung eines gemeinen Kastens. Ratschlag, wie die geistlichen Güter zu handeln sind. (Establishment of a Common Fund. Advice on How to Handle Ecclesiastical Property.) Wittenberg, 1523. 12 leaves. 20 x 15.5 cm.
A: Title page
On the use of Church property for schools and caring for the poor.

25.
LUTHER, MARTIN: An die Ratsherren aller Städte deutsches Landes: daß sie christliche Schulen aufrichten und halten sollen. (Call to the Councilmen of All Cities of Germany to Erect and Maintain Christian Schools.) Wittenberg, 1524. 19 leaves. 21 x 15 cm.
A: Title page
A declaration of belief in the humanistic ideal of education.

26.
Handlung, Artikel und Instruction von allen Rotten und Haufen der Bauern. (Act, Articles and Instruction Concerning All Gangs and Mobs of Farmers.) 1525. 6 leaves. 18 x 14 cm.
A: Title page
Twelve articles by the Swabian peasants made during the Peasant's War, 1524–1526.

27.
LUTHER, MARTIN: Wider die mörderischen und räuberischen Rotten der Bauern. (Against the Murdering and Robbing Gangs of Farmers.) Wittenberg, 1525. 4 leaves. 20 x 15 cm.
A: Title page
Call on rulers to put down the revolt.

28.
Sächsisches Stammbuch. Sammlung von Bildnissen sächsischer Fürsten. (Saxon Genealogy. Collection of Portraits of Saxon Electors.) c. 1550. 116 leaves. 42 x 28 cm.
A: The electors Friedrich the Wise and Johann the Constant
The album extends from the electors of legendary times to Elector Moritz of Saxony.

29.
LUTHER, MARTIN: Deutsche Messe und Ordnung des Gottesdienstes. (German Masses and Order of the Worship Service.) Wittenberg, 1526. 24 leaves. 18 x 14 cm.
A: Title page
Renewal of the worship service.

30.
LUTHER, MARTIN: Trostschrift an die Christen zu Halle. Eigenhändiges Manuskript. (Consolation for the Christians of Halle. Autograph manuscript.) Wittenberg, 1527. 62 leaves. 21 x 16 cm.
A: Leaf 11a
Codex, with manuscripts by Martin Luther.

31.
LUTHER, MARTIN: Trostschrift an die Christen zu Halle. (Consolation for the Christians of Halle.) Wittenberg, 1527. 14 leaves. 18 x 15 cm.
A: Title page
Printed copy of the manuscript shown as item 30.

32.
LUTHER, MARTIN: Deutscher Katechismus. (German Catechism.) Wittenberg, 1530. 75 leaves. 19 x 15.5 cm.
A: Leaves 42b–43a
Instruction for Protestant pastors.

33.
LUTHER, MARTIN: Enchiridion. Der kleine Katechismus. (Enchiridion. The Small Catechism.) Leipzig, 1561. 140 leaves. 16 x 11 cm.
A: Leaf 70b
The sacrament of baptism.

34. *See figure 8.*
LUTHER, MARTIN: Autograph letter to Duchess Katharina of Saxony. Wittenberg, 28 July 1539. 1 leaf. 33 x 21.5 cm.
A: Autograph letter
Letter from Luther to Duchess Katharina of Saxony.

35.
Imagines Electorum Saxoniae. (Images of the Electors of Saxony.) Wittenberg, 1570. 11 leaves. 20 x 15.5 cm.
A: Portrait of Elector Johann Friedrich the Magnanimous
Luther's regent and a defender of the Reformation.

36.
MELANCHTHON, PHILIPP: Autograph letter to Nikolaus von Amsdorf. 23 September 1546. 1 leaf. 32 x 21.5 cm.
Melanchthon (1497–1560) and Amsdorf (1483–1565) were Luther's closest colleagues.

37.
SPANGENBERG, JOHANN: Evangelisches Kirchengesangbuch. (Protestant Hymnal.) Magdeburg, 1545. 718 leaves. 33 x 24 cm.
A: Pages 532–533
Earliest and most important collection of liturgical music for the Protestant religious service.

38.
Das Leben und die ganze evangelische Historie von Jesu Christo. (The Life and Complete Protestant History of Jesus Christ.) Sixteenth century. Vellum. 118 leaves. 19 x 14 cm.
A: Leaves 60b–61a
Prayer book with colored woodcuts from the time of Dürer.

The Bible

39.
L'apocalipse mon seigneur S. Jehan. (The Apocalypse of My Lord Saint John.) France, fourteenth century. Vellum. 56 leaves. 25 x 20 cm.
A: Leaves 33b–34a
The Apocalypse of Saint John, with 72 miniatures from a Lotharingian scriptorium.

40.
The New Testament in the English Translation by John Wycliffe. England, beginning of fifteenth century. Vellum. 414 leaves. 18 x 15 cm.
A: Pages 326–327
John Wycliffe (c. 1328–84) translated the Bible into colloquial English.

41.
Deutsche Historienbibel. (German Historical Bible.) Germany, beginning of fifteenth century. 282 leaves. 42 x 32.5 cm.
A: Pages 138–139
Popular treatment of biblical texts.

42.
Biblia. Mit Glossen nach den Postillen des Nicolaus von Lyra. Niederdeutsch. (The Bible. With commentaries based on the Postillae of Nicholas of Lyra. Low German.) Cologne, c. 1478. 514 leaves. 37 x 29 cm.
A: Job/Proverbs
Early Low German printing of the Bible by Heinrich Quentell, with 123 colored woodcuts.

43. *See figure 9.*
Biblia. (The Bible.) Venice, 1479. 451 leaves. Vellum. 34 x 23.5 cm.
A: Beginning of Genesis
A Bible printed by Nikolaus Jenson.

44.
Biblia polyglotta Hebraica, Chaldaica, Graeca et Latina. (Polyglot Bible in Hebrew, Chaldaic, Greek, and Latin.) Vol. 1. Alcalá de Henares, Spain, 1514. 300 leaves. 37 x 30 cm.
A: Leaf xii
Printing of the 600 copies of this Bible cost 50,000 gold guilders.

45.
Novum Testamentum omne ab Erasmo Roterdamo. (Complete New Testament by Erasmus of Rotterdam.) Basel, 1519. 566 leaves. 34 x 24 cm.
A: Leaves 110–111, Beginning of the Gospel of Matthew
Translation by Erasmus of the original Greek text. Luther translated the New Testament from this.

46.
Das Neue Testament deutsch. In der Übersetzung von Martin Luther. (The New Testament in German. Translated by Martin Luther.) Wittenberg, 1522. 203 leaves. 29 x 20.5 cm.
A: Leaves n1b–n2a
The translation was made in only eleven weeks, during Luther's stay at Wartburg Castle in 1521–22.

47.
Die ganze Bibel, das ist alle Bücher Altes und Neues Testament. (The Entire Bible, That Is, Every Book of the Old and New Testaments.) Zurich, 1531. 334, 315 leaves. 37 x 26 cm.
A: Pages 228–29
Deluxe edition of the Zurich Bible, with illustrations by Hans Holbein the Younger (1497–1543).

48. *See figure 10.*
Biblia deutsch. Übersetzt von Martin Luther. (The Bible in German. Translated by Martin Luther.) Wittenberg, 1534. 928 leaves. 30 x 26.5 cm.
A: Frontispiece and title page
Luther's German Translation of the Bible.

49.
Biblia, das ist die ganze Heilige Schrift deutsch. (The Bible, That Is, the Entire Holy Scripture in German.) Frankfurt am Main, 1561. 410 leaves. 40 x 28 cm.
A: Leaf 241a, Beginning of the New Testament
The woodcuts were created by the Nuremberg artist Virgil Solis (1514–1568).

50.
Biblia. Die ganze Heilige Schrift D. Martin Lutheri. (The Bible. The Entire Holy Scripture of Martin Luther.) Lüneburg, 1665. 302, 198, 160 leaves. 43.5 x 30.5 cm.
A: Plates to leaves 32–33
Artistically the most splendid Bible of the baroque era.

51.
The Bible in the Language of the Delawares. Cambridge, 1680. 602 leaves. 19 x 15.5 cm.
A: Leaf 1a, Beginning of the New Testament.
John Eliot's Indian language Bible.

The Electoral Library

52. *See figure 11.*
Biblia Germanico-Latina. (German-Latin Bible.) Wittenberg, 1565. 162 leaves. Printed on vellum. 21 x 15.5 cm.
A: Portrait of Elector Augustus
Personal Bible of Elector Augustus the Strong.

53.
Matthioli, Petrus Andreas: Commentarii. (Commentaries.) Venice, 1554. 149 leaves. 34 x 24 cm.
Binding from 1556, the year of the establishment of the Saxon State Library; with the supralibros: A(ugust) H(erzog) Z(u) S(achsen) K(urfürst)

54.
Katalog der Bibliothek des Kurfürsten August. (Catalog of the Library of Elector Augustus.) 1580. 90 leaves. 31.5 x 20.5 cm.
A: Pages 23–24
The handwritten catalog lists 2,354 works from all fields of knowledge.

55.
Agricola, Georg: Bergwerkbuch (Mining Book.) Frankfurt am Main, 1580. 491 leaves. 31 x 22 cm.
A: Pages 152–53
First comprehensive treatise on the mining industry.

56.
Tables on the Release of the Saxon Electoral Coin. Dresden, 1583. 301 leaves. 37 x 27.5 cm.
A: Pages 70–71
Account of Saxon mining output for 1568.

57. *See figure 12.*
Kentmann, Johannes: Kräuterbuch. (Book of Herbs.) 1563. 299 leaves. 50 x 40 cm.
A: Leaves 146b–47a
An early illustration of American tomato plants, entitled "Red Apples from the New World."

58.
Bartisch, Georg: Kunstbuch, darinnen ist der ganze gründliche Bericht des Blasensteines. (Art Book Containing a Thorough Report on Kidney Stones.) 1575. 239 leaves. 31 x 22.5 cm.
A: Leaves 135b–36a
Manuscript of the oldest German urological text of scientific quality.

59.
Vesalius, Andreas: De humani corporis fabrica. (On the Structure of the Human Body.) Basel, 1543. 659 leaves. 43.5 x 32.5 cm.
A: Pages 162–63
Vesalius's pioneering sixteenth-century atlas on anatomy.

60. *See figure 13.*
Mair, Paulus Hector: Fecht-, Ring- und Turnierbuch. (Book of Fencing, Wrestling, and Jousting.) Mid-sixteenth century. 242 leaves. 41 x 30 cm.
A: Leaves 77b–78a
A treatise on fencing, wrestling, and jousting.

61. *See figure 14.*
Senftenberg, Veit Wolff von: Kriegserfindungen. (Military Inventions.) Second half of sixteenth century. 173 leaves. 23 x 18.5 cm.
A: Leaves 97b–98a
An important treatise on the invention and use of weaponry.

62. *See figure 15.*
Loeneyss, Georg Engelhart: Gründlicher Bericht und Ordnung der Gebisse. (Thorough Report on Equestrian Dentistry.) 1576. 249 leaves. 51 x 39 cm.
A: Leaves 22b–23a
A treatise on horses, their handling, and equipage.

63.
Örtung der Reise von Mühlberg bis Regensburg. (Itinerary of the Journey from Mühlberg to Regensburg.) 1575. Vellum scroll. 11 x 1380 cm.
Elector Augustus's route for his trip to the Reichstag in Regensburg in the fall of 1575.

64.
Unterricht, wie man das Vaterunser beten soll. (Instruction for Praying the Lord's Prayer) 1561. 81 leaves. Vellum. 17 x 11.5 cm.
A: Leaves 32b–33a
Prayer book belonging to Elector Augustus.

65.
Sachs, Hans: Meistergesangbuch. (Master Hymnal.) c. 1560. 228 leaves. 22 x 34 cm.
A: Leaves 11b–12a
Autograph manuscript by the greatest and most prolific German poet of the sixteenth century.

66.
Funeral Procession of Elector August from Dresden to Freiberg, 14 March 1586. Folding sheet. 24 x 51 cm.
A: Page 11

67. *See figure 16.*
Harriot, Thomas: Customs of the Savages in Virginia. Frankurt am Main, 1590. 66 leaves. 34 x 25 cm.
A: Leaves 47b–48a
The city of Secotá.

68. *See figure 17.*
Bretschneider, Daniel: Ein Buch von allerlei Inventionen zu Schlittenfahrten. (A Book of Various Inventions for Sled Travel.) Dresden, 1602. 51 leaves. 16 x 38 cm.
A: Leaf 36

69. *See figure 18.*
Tierhatz auf dem Altmarkt zu Dresden. (Animal Chase in the Old Market in Dresden.) 1609. 8 leaves. 46 x 60 cm.
A: Leaf 2
Pictures depicting various types of hunts staged at carnival time

Fine Renaissance Bindings

70. *See figure 19.*
Division Tables. c. 1570. Part 2. 1,000 tables. 16 x 21 cm.

71. *See figure 20.*
Paul, Simon: Postilla. Magdeburg, 1572. 512 leaves. 17 x 11 cm.

72.
Fischer, Christoph: Von dem hochwürdigen Abendmahl. (From the Last Supper.) Uelzen, 1575. 211 leaves. 17 x 11 cm.
Calf binding by Jakob Krause with Moorish ornamentation in gilt.

73.
Peucer, Caspar: Das fünfte Buch der Chronica Carionis (The Fifth Book of the Chronicles of Carion.) Dresden, 1576. Pages 209–435, 58 leaves. 39 x 26 cm.
Deluxe edition by Jakob Krause with the coat of arms of the electorate of Saxony.

74. *See figure 21.*
Betbüchlein für allerlei Anliegen. (Small Prayer Book for All Occasions.) c. 1580. 131 leaves. 21 x 20 cm.

75.
Miltitz, Nicol von, and Georg Rudolf Marschalk: Roßarznei-Buch. (Equine Veterinary Book.) Dresden, 1589. 225 leaves. Vellum. 33 x 23 cm.
Gilt cordovan binding by Caspar Meuser, with silver clasps.

76.
Franz, Paul: Christliche nützliche Fragen. (Useful Christian Questions.) 1590. 15 leaves, 498 pages. 18 x 12 cm.
Painted gilt binding by Caspar Meuser, with Saxon and Brandenburg coats of arms.

The Electoral Hofkapelle

77.
Amann, Jost, and Georg Gärtner: Heidnischer Stamm des hochlöblichen Hauses zu Sachsen. (The Pagan Roots of the Noble House of Saxony.) c. 1650. 55 leaves.
A: Leaves 49b–50a, portrait
Elector Moritz (1521–53), founder of the Hofkapelle.

78.
Walter, Johann: Von den Zeichen des Tags ein schön Lied. (From the Signs of the Day a Beautiful Song.) Text by Erasmus Albe. 1548. Folding sheet. 18.5 x 15 cm.
A: Pages 2–3
Unknown composition of 1548, the founding year of the Hofkapelle, by Johann Walter, first cantor and choirmaster and a friend of Luther.

79.
Bercht, Friedrich: Gemalte Aufzüge. (Painted Processions.) Dresden, 1581. 2 leaves. Gouache painting. 34 x 48 cm.
The court trumpeters were the highest ranking musicians in Germany, since Elector August occupied the position of grand marshal.

80. *See figure 22.*
Bretschneider, Daniel: Contrafactur des Ringrennens und anderer Ritterspiele auf Christians fürstlichem Beilager am 25. April Anno [15]82 in Dresden. (Contrafactum of the Ring Competition and Other Knightly Games at the Princely Consummation of Christian's Marriage on April 25 of the Year [15]82 in Dresden.) Dresden, c. 1582. 67 leaves. 25.5 x 55.5 cm.
A: The fourth part

81.
Scandelli, Antonio: Gaudii Paschalis Jesu Christi redivivi … relatio historica. (Historical Account of the Easter Joy of the Resurrected Jesus Christ.) Edited and published by Samuel Besler. Breslau, 1612. 22 leaves. 30.5 x 20.5 cm.
A: Page 5
Posthumous edition of a work that was atypical for the time, by the first Italian director of the Hofkapelle.

82.
Pinelli, Giovanni Battista: Deutsches Magnificat. (German Magnificat.) Tenor part book. Dresden, 1583. 134 leaves. 15 x 20 cm.
A: Page 2, with a portrait of the composer
Rare edition of the German-language compositions by the second Italian director of the Hofkapelle.

83.
ALBRICI, VINCENZO: Missa in C für 5 Singstimmen, Streicher, 4 Trompeten und Pauken. (Mass in C for Five Voices, Strings, Four Trumpets and Tympani.) Manuscript score. Dresden, end of seventeenth century. 42 leaves. 31 x 20.5 cm.
A: Pages 12–13
At the head of the score is a notation: Sig. Vicentius Albrici. S(erenissimi): E(lectoris): S(axoniae): C(apellae): M(agister).

84.
NAUWACH, JOHANN: Erster Teil Deutscher Villanellen mit 1, 2 und 3 Stimmen, auf die Tiorba, Laute, Clavicymbel und andere Instrumente gerichtet. (First Part of German Villanellas, with 1, 2, and 3 voices; with accompaniment for a theorbo, lute, harpsichord, and other instruments.) Dresden, 1627. 23 leaves. 28 x 18 cm.
A: Title page
Rarity from the earliest collections of the Music Department of the Saxon State Library, with presentation inscription to Elector Johann Georg I.

85.
SCHÜTZ, HEINRICH: Königs und Propheten David Hundertneunzehnter Psalm. (The 119th Psalm of David, the King and Prophet.) Manuscript part for Cantus 1; with printed title page. Dresden, 1671. 20 leaves. 27.5 x 19.5 cm.
A: Title page
A vocal score from the only source collecting the last works of Schütz, with notation on the title page in Schütz's own hand.

86.
BONTEMPI, GIOVANNI, AND GIUSEPPE PERANDA: Drama oder Musikalisches Schauspiel von der Dafne. (Musical play on the legend of Daphne.) Manuscript fair copy. Dresden, 1671–72. 116 leaves. 23.5 x 34 cm.
A: Title page
Source for the opera Daphne.

87.
Opera-Ballett von dem Judicio Paridis und der Helena Raub. (Opera Ballet of the Judgment of Paris and the Rape of Helen.) Dresden, 1679. 18 leaves, 10 engravings. 30 x 19 cm.
A: Stage view
Text edition with eight scene designs and two interior views of the opera house erected by Wolf Caspar von Klengel.

88.
DEDEKIND, CONSTANTIN CHRISTIAN: Aelbianische Musenlust, in unterschiedlicher berühmter Poeten auserlesenen, mit anmutigen Melodien beseelten, Lust-, Ehren-, Zucht- und Tugendliedern. (Albion Fancy of the Muses, in Songs of Merriment, Honor, Discipline and Virtue. Selected from Various Famous Poets and Animated by Charming Melodies.) Dresden, 1657. 205 leaves. 15.5 x 18.5 cm.
A: Engraved title page
Presumably the only complete copy of the collected songs of the Dresden virtuoso concertmaster, Constantin Dedekind.

Twilight of a Century

89. *See figure 23.*
Collection of Portraits of the Counts of Saxony. Seventeenth century. 52 miniatures on vellum. 47 x 29 cm.
A: Leaf 48

90.
DE WIT, FREDERIK: Karte von Deutschland. (Map of Germany.) c. 1680. Silk. Hand-colored print. 62 x 70 cm.

91.
Old Dresden and Dresden with the Elbe Bridge. c. 1650. Engraving. 58 x 82 cm.

92.
WECK, ANTON: Der Kurfürstlichen sächsischen Residenz und Hauptfestung Dresden Beschreibung und Vorstellung. (Description and View of the Residence of the Elector of Saxony and the Main Fortress of Dresden.) Nuremberg, 1680. 552 pages, 8 leaves. 45 x 41.5 cm.
A: Plate 12
The Kurfürstliche Bibliothek (Electoral Library) was located here from 1556 until the castle fire of 1701.

93.
ZSCHIMMER, GABRIEL: Durchlauchtigste Zusammenkunft. (The Most Serene Meeting.) Nuremberg, 1680. Engraving. 37 x 120 cm.

A: Plate 2, page 20

Procession of citizens through Wilsdruffer Street, from the Old Marketplace to Wilis Gate in Dresden.

94.
SCHEIN, JOHANN HERMANN: Allegrezza sprirituale … auf das Jubelfest der Evangelischen Lutherischen Kirchen. Mit acht Stimmen samt Generalbass. Stimme Basso continuo. (Allegrezza spirituale … at the Jubilee Celebration of the Protestant Lutheran Churches. In eight vocal parts with bass continuo. Bass continuo part.) Leipzig, 1617. 86 leaves. 31 x 20 cm.

A: Title page

Celebratory motet by the cantor of the St. Thomas Church of Leipzig, on the hundredth anniversary of the circulation of Luther's theses in Wittenberg.

95. a, b
KNÜPFER, SEBASTIAN: Wer ist der, so von Edom kommt. Dialogus Festo Paschatos accommodatus, a 15, 20, 30 vocibus. (Who Is He Who Comes from Edom. Dialogue Suited for an Easter Celebration, for 15, 20, 30 voices.) Copyist score by Samuel Jacobi. 1676. 14 leaves. 31.5 x 19.5 cm.

A: Cover and page 1

An important work by the cantor of the St. Thomas Church in a seventeenth-century copyist manuscript.

96.
SCHELLE, JOHANN: Ich lebe und ihr sollt auch leben. Geistliches Konzert für Basso solo und Instrumente. 10 Stimmen, geschrieben v. Samuel Jacobi. (I Live and You Shall Also Live. Sacred Concert for Solo Bass and Instruments. Ten parts; written by Samuel Jacobi.) Grimma, last quarter of seventeenth century. 11 leaves. 20 x 16.5 cm.

A: All vocals broken down into parts

The works of Cantor Johann Schelle of the St. Thomas Church in Leipzig survive today only in the Saxon State Library.

97.
KUHNAU, JOHANN: Was Gott tut, das ist wohlgetan. Kirchenkantate für Soli, Chor und Instrumente. Stimmenmaterial von der Hand Johann Gottfried Schichts. 27 Stimmen. (Whatever God Does Is Well Done. Church Cantata for Solo, Choir, and Instruments. Vocal material from the hand of Johann Gottfried Schicht. 27 parts.) End of eighteenth to beginning of nineteenth century. 33 leaves. 31 x 23 cm.

A: All vocals broken down into parts

A work by Kuhnau, J. S. Bach's predecessor, transcribed by Bach's fifth successor, Schicht.

98.
Corpus iuris Saxonici. (Electoral Saxon Ordinances, Constitutions, Mandates, Patents, and Rights.) Dresden, 1673. 34 x 22.5 cm.

A: Title page

The first printed collection of the laws of the state of Saxony.

99.
Täglich neu einlaufende Kriegs- und Welthändel. (Daily New Incoming Military and Global Transactions.) Leipzig, 1660. 1,392 pages, 8 leaves. 20 x 18.5 cm.

A: Pages 604–605

First year's issues of the oldest German daily newspaper.

100.
Acta eruditorum. (Activities of Scholars.) Year 1. Leipzig, 1682. 402 pages, 6 leaves. 22 x 17 cm.

A: Pages 160–61

First year's issues of the oldest German scholarly journal.

101.
Von Schießen und Feuerwerk (Büchsenmeisterei). (On Shooting and Fireworks.) Seventeenth century. 140 pages, 63 leaves. 20 x 18.5 cm.

A: Plate 7

The production of gunpowder.

102.
Propheten, Apokryphen und Neues Testament. Übersetzt von Martin Luther. (Prophets, Apocrypha, and New Testament. Translated by Martin Luther.) Wittenberg, 1572. 470 leaves. 41 x 29 cm.

The Bible of Elector Johann Georg I (ruled 1611–56), with chased and fire-gilded brass binding.

103. *See figure 24.*
Biblia. Übersetzt von Martin Luther. (The Bible. Translated by Martin Luther.) Nuremberg, 1652. 416 pages, 90 leaves. 48 x 35 cm.
A: Cover
Bible of Elector Moritz of Sachsen-Zeitz, with his coat of arms.

104.
Das unschuldige Leiden ... Jesu Christi. (The Innocent Suffering ... of Jesus Christ.) Dresden, 1653. 154 leaves. Vellum. 15.5 x 13 cm.
A: Leaves 77b–78a
Prayer book of Elector Johann Georg I.

The Augustan Era

105.
Großes vollständiges Universal-Lexikon. (Great Complete Universal Dictionary.) Vol. 3. Halle, Leipzig, 1733. 2,000 columns, 7 leaves. 35 x 23 cm.
A: Portrait of Friedrich August I

106.
Biblia sacra. (Sacred Bible.) Nuremberg, 1714. 520 pages, 12 leaves. 30 x 22 cm.
Binding with the coat of arms of August the Strong, Polish king and elector of Saxony.

107.
Friedrich August I, Elector of Saxony and King of Poland: Letter to Count-Palatine of Livonia Karlsbad, 12 June 1717. 2 leaves. 23 x 17.5 cm.
To majordomo Josef Kos, tutor of the crown prince.

108. *See figure 25.*
Atlas Royal. Vol. 1. Amsterdam, 1707. 3, 73 leaves. 65 x 55 cm.

109. *See figure 26.*
Pöppelmann, Matthäus Daniel: Entwurf für einen Zwingerpavillon. (Draft for a Zwinger pavilion.) Dresden, 1712–13. Colored sketch. 41.5 x 28 cm.

110.
Pöppelmann, Matthäus Daniel: Ehrentempel zum Fest des 49. Geburtstages Friedrich August I. (Pantheon for the Festival of the Forty-ninth Birthday of Friedrich August I.) Dresden, 1718. Colored drawing. 45 x 41.5 cm.

111.
Costume Figures for a Masquerade. Eighteenth century. 43 leaves. 53 x 38 cm.
A: Plates 14, 15

112.
Heinichen, Johann David: Flavio Crispo. Dramma per musica in 3. Atti, Band 3. Abschrift (unvollendet). (Flavio Crispo. Musical drama in three acts, Vol. 3. Copyist's manuscript (incomplete).) Dresden, 1720. 84 leaves. 26 x 31 cm.
A: Pages 134–135
Unique transmission of the last opera by the Dresden court musical director.

113.
Vivaldi, Antonio: Concerto fatto per il M[aestr]o Pisendel. (Concerto composed for M[aestr]o Pisendel). Autograph score with ornamental sketches by Pisendel. Venice and Dresden, between 1717 and 1730. 12 leaves. 24 x 32.5 cm.
A: Pages 10, 11, 11a
Impressive testimony to the creative collaboration between Vivaldi and the Dresden musical director Pisendel.

114.
Pisendel, Johann Georg: First Movement of a Violin Concerto, with corrections in Vivaldi's Hand. Autograph score. Venice, c. 1717. 5 leaves. 23 x 31.5 cm.
A: Page 6
Clear evidence that Pisendel was a student of Vivaldi.

115.
Zelenka, Jan Dismas: Requiem für Friedrich August I. von Sachsen und Polen. (Requiem for Frederik Augustus I of Saxony and Poland.) Autograph score. Dresden, 1733. 7 leaves (1 fascicle). 35.5 x 23.5 cm.
A: Page 1
Splendid documentation of the abilities of the Hofkapelle at that time.

116.
Weiss, Silvius Leopold: Lautenkompositionen in französischer Tabulaturschrift. (Compositions for Lute in French Tablature.) Vol. 6. Title in composer's hand. 1731. 35 leaves. 25 x 33 cm.
A: Pages 8 and 9
Autograph manuscript of the most significant lutist of the time.

117. *See figure 27.*
Bach, Johann Sebastian: Missa (h moll: Kyrie und Gloria). Originaler Stimmensatz. (Mass in B Minor: Kyrie and Gloria. Original Vocal Part.) Leipzig, 1733. 2 leaves. 40 x 30 cm.
A: Bass voice (composer's autograph)
Manuscript score.

118.
Harrer, Johann Gottlieb: Missa in D. (Mass in D.) Autograph score. Dresden, 1738. 88 leaves. 33.5 x 16.5 cm.
A: Pages 156–157, with corrections by Zelenka
Harrer was Bach's successor as cantor of the St. Thomas Church in Leipzig, and was previously in the service of Count Brühl in Dresden.

119.
Hasse, Johann Adolf: Ipermestra. Dramma per musica in 3 Atti. (Ipermestra. Musical drama in three acts.) Text by Pietro Metastasio. Copy of the score with autograph additions and corrections. Dresden, c. 1745–50. 177 leaves. 22.5 x 31 cm.
A: Pages 122–123
The unperformed intermediate version between the 1744 Vienna performance and the 1751 Dresden performance.

120.
Maria Antonia Walpurgis, Electoress of Saxony: Il Trionfo della fedelta. Dramma per musica in 3 Atti. (The Triumph of Fidelity. Musical drama in three acts.) Lyrics by the composer.
a) Copyist's score. Vol. 2. Dresden, mid-eighteenth century. 64 leaves. 23 x 30.5 cm.
b) Cadenza to an aria of the second act, for soprano and oboe (autograph). Dresden, mid-eighteenth century. 2 leaves. 24 x 32 cm.
A: Pages 106–107; page 2
Author's copy with additions in her own hand.

121.
Bellotto, Bernardo (Canaletto): Hofkirche. (Court Church.) Eighteenth century. Engraving. 40 x 50 cm.

122.
Bellotto, Bernardo (Canaletto): Zwingerhof (Zwinger Court.) Eighteenth century. Engraving. 40 x 50 cm.
View of the pavilions where the Electoral Library was located from 1728 to 1786.

123. *See figure 28.*
Merian, Maria Sibylla: Metamorphosis insectorum Surinamensium. (Metamorphosis of the Insects of Surinam.) Amsterdam, 1705. 2, 60 pages, 60 plates. 58 x 44 cm.
A: Figure 46

124.
Leibniz, Gottfried Wilhelm von: Theodicaea. Amsterdam, 1726. 552 pages. 18 x 11 cm.
A: Title page
Chief work of this philosopher and versatile scholar who was born in Leipzig.

125.
Moritz, Count of Saxony: Des reveries. (Musings.) 1732. 319 pages, 85 plates. 43 x 29 cm.
A: Page 100, plate 40
Military compendium by Count Moritz of Saxony, son of August the Strong and Countess Aurora of Königsmark.

126.
Barre, P.: Histoire générale d'Allemagne. (General History of Germany.). Vol. 8. Paris, 1748. Pages 785–1128, pages 1–344, 24 leaves. 30 x 23.5 cm.
A: v. 8, cover
Morocco binding with the supralibros of Friedrich August II, Polish king and elector of Saxony (1696–1763).

127.
Heraldic Description of the Coat of Arms of the Elector of Saxony. Eighteenth century. 13 plates, 27 leaves. 21 x 17.5 cm.
A: Leaf 1b
Gouache drawing and written description.

128.
Bünau, Heinrich von: Deutsche Kaiser- und Reichshistorie. (History of the German Emperors and of the German Empire.) Vol. 1. Leipzig, 1728. 925 pages, 28 leaves. 28 x 21 cm.
A: Frontispiece, title page
Reference work on German history, of which four volumes were published.

129.
Pontas, Johannes: Dictionarium. (Dictionary.) Vol. 1. Luxemburg, 1731. 546 pages, 8 leaves. 42 x 28 cm.
A: Cover, gilt-embossed leather
Binding with supralibros of Count Heinrich von Bünau. His comprehensive library of 42,000 volumes was incorporated into the electoral collection in 1765.

130.
Großes vollständiges Universal-Lexikon (Great Complete Universal Encyclopedia.) Vol. 27. Leipzig, Halle, 1741. 5 leaves, 2,246 columns. 35 x 23 cm.
A: Frontispiece, title page
Oldest modern encyclopedia of Germany, in 68 volumes. On the engraved title page: the Saxon Prime Minister, Count Heinrich von Brühl, whose collection of 62,000 volumes was purchased for the electoral collection in 1768.

131.
Pontas, Johannes: Dictionarium. (Dictionary.) Vol. 2. Venice, 1744. 711 pages. 36 x 25 cm. (closed.)
A: Cover
Supralibros of Count Heinrich von Brühl.

132.
Seutter, Matthias: Stadtplan von Dresden. (City Map of Dresden.) 1755. Colored engraving. 61 x 75 cm.
The fortress-like character of both parts of the city can be seen.

133.
Portrait of Graf Nikolaus Ludwig von Zinzendorf. 1755. Engraving. 23 x 16 cm.
Founder of the Moravian Church.

134.
Zinzendorf, Graf Nikolaus Ludwig von: Autograph manuscript of his "Theologische Bedenken." (Theological Reflections.) Herrnhut, 13 January 1733. 2 leaves. 19 x 31.5 cm.
Part of the original manuscript in Zinzendorf's own hand.

135.
Veith, J. P.: Herrnhut. Ansicht von Süden. (Herrnhut. View from the South.) End of eighteenth century. Watercolor drawing. 59 x 70 cm.
Herrnhut is the location where the defunct Moravian religion was revived.

136.
The Daily Recitations of the Moravian Church for the Year 1776. Barby, 1775. 76 leaves. 18 x 11 cm.
First edition of the Moravians' recitations with instructional texts.

The Frauenkirche

137.
Dresden. Neumarkt with the Frauenkirche. Second half of eighteenth century. Watercolor, pen and ink drawing. 72 x 51 cm.

138. *See figure 29.*
Plans et élévations des différentes églises. (Plans and Elevations of Various Churches.) First half of eighteenth century. Colored pen and ink drawing. 48 x 56 cm.
Original cross-sectional drawing of the Frauenkirche.

139. *See figure 30.*
Wagner, Richard: Das Liebesmahl der Apostel. Biblische Szene für Männerstimmen und großes Orchester. (The Love Feast of the Apostles. Biblical Scene for Male Voices and Large Orchestra.) Autograph score. Dresden, 1843. 31 leaves. 34 x 27 cm.
A: Pages 22–23
Original score.

140.
Ringing of the Frauenkirche Bells in Dresden. Original recording. Direct cut on Decelith. Cassette recording in exhibit. Dresden, c. 1940. Diameter 30 cm.
Recording of the bells destroyed in 1945.

141. *See figure 31.*
Reinhold, Friedrich Johann Christian: Uniformen der kurfürstlich sächsischen Armee. (Uniforms of the Army of the Electorate of Saxony.) 1791. 31 leaves. 15.4 x 23 cm.
A: Leaf 15 (26)
Illustrations of the Elector's army.

142.
Dresden. Panoramic View from the Cupola of the Frauenkirche. 1824. Colored lithograph. 62 x 60 cm.
"Fish-eye" view of Dresden.

The Age of Goethe

143. *See figure 32.*
Dresden. View of the City from the Southwest. End of eighteenth century. Colored engraving. 66 x 81 cm.

144. *See figure 33.*
Winckelmann, Johann Joachim: Gedanken über die Nachahmung der griechischen Werke. (Thoughts on the Imitation of Greek Works.) Friedrichstadt near Dresden, 1755. 40 pages, 4 leaves. 25 x 21.5 cm.
A: Title page
A pioneering essay in the establishment of modern scientific archaeology and art history.

145.
Portrait of Johann Joachim Winckelmann (1717–89). c. 1760. Engraving. 25 x 19.5 cm.
Founder of modern aesthetics.

146.
Goethe, Johann Wolfgang von: Die Leiden des jungen Werthers. (The Sorrows of Young Werther.) Leipzig, 1774. 224 pages. 16.5 x 9.5 cm.
A: Title page
An eighteenth-century best seller. This is the rare anonymously issued first edition.

147. *See figure 34.*
Goethe, Johann Wolfgang von: Letter to Johann Gottlob von Quandt. Weimar, 9 June 1831. 2 leaves, wrapper. 25.5 x 21 cm.
Regarding paintings coming from Dresden to Weimar.

148.
Dresden. Japanese Palace. 1795. Watercolor drawing. 55 x 80 cm.
Location of the Royal Library from 1786 to 1945, built by the famous architect Matthäus Daniel Pöppelmann.

149.
Schiller, Friedrich von: Die Räuber. (The Robbers.) Leipzig, 1781. Collection: 32, 222, 130, 96, 108, 127 pages. 18 x 11 cm.
A: Title page
The most significant drama of the Sturm und Drang *period in eighteenth-century German literature.*

150.
Schiller, Friedrich von: Autograph Letter to Christian Körner. Rudolstadt, 1 September 1788. 2 leaves.
This letter from Schiller to Körner discusses personal and aesthetic matters.

151.
Hiller, Johann Adam: Die Liebe auf dem Lande. Singspiel in 3 Akten. (Love in the Country. Singspiel in three acts.) Autograph score, fair copy. Leipzig, c. 1768. 125 leaves. 20 x 26 cm.
A: Pages 28–29
Hiller was the cantor of the St. Thomas Church in Leipzig, a versatile musical organizer and writer on musical subjects, known as the representative of the middle German Singspiel.

152.
Naumann, Johann Gottlieb: Gustaf Wasa. Tragisk opera i 3 acter (Gustaf Vasa. Tragic opera in three acts.) Autograph score. Vol. 2. Stockholm, 1782–83. 97 leaves. 24.5 x 34 cm.
A: Page 185
This work, commissioned for the musical director of the Saxon court, is still regarded as the Swedish national opera.

153.
Gli Amanti folletti. Dramma buffo in due Atti. (The Lover Imps. Comic opera in two acts.) Libretto. Fair copy, with autograph corrections by Prince Anton of Saxony. Dresden, c. 1793. 41 leaves. 24.5 x 18 cm.
A: Leaves 12b–13a
This opera, performed in Dresden, was compiled from various works by Mozart.

154.
Paer, Ferdinando: L'Amante servitor. Dramma giocoso per musica in 2 atti. (The Servant Lover. Comic opera in two acts.) Autograph score of the opening symphony. Venice, 1796 (or Dresden, after 1801). 20 leaves. 21.5 x 30 cm.
A: Page 1
Napoleon lured the Dresden music director to Paris in 1807.

155.
Ebert, Friedrich Adolf: The First Subject Catalog "Musik" of the Royal Public Library in Dresden. Autograph fair copy. Dresden, 1816. 89 leaves. 33.5 x 21 cm.
A: Pages 14–15
The first catalog "Musik" of the Royal Public Library was established.

156.
Mersenne, Martin: Harmonie universelle, contenant la théorie et la pratique de la musique. (Universal Harmony, Containing the Theory and Practice of Music.) Paris, 1636–37. 782 pages, 2 leaves. 36 x 23 cm.
A: Main title and table of contents
One of the earliest acquisitions of the Music Department; with detailed table of contents by Chief Librarian Friedrich Adolf Ebert.

Romanticism in Dresden

157.
Tibullus, Albius: Elegiarum libri quatuor. (Four Books of Elegies.) Venice, 1520. 179 leaves. 31 x 22 cm.
A: Cover
Binding with supralibros of Elector Friedrich August III (1750–1827), who after 1806 was King Friedrich August I of Saxony.

158.
Schloß Pillnitz. (Pillnitz Castle.) c. 1800. Colored engraving. 37 x 47 cm.
Summer residence of the House of Wettin since the eighteenth century.

159. *See figure 35.*
Plantae selectae vivis coloribus depictae. (Selected Plants Shown in True-to-Life Colors.) Centuria 1. 1785–95. 100 leaves. 53 x 40 cm.
A: Plate 22
One of hundreds of plants grown st Pillnitz castle.

160.
Portrait of Carl Maria von Weber. 1823. Lithograph. 35 x 23 cm.
Weber's works inspired the Romantic movement in German opera.

161.
Weber, Carl Maria von: Jubel-Ouverture. Zur Feier des 50 jährigen Regierungsantritts Sr. Maj. des Königs von Sachsen d. 20. September 1818 (Overture of Jubilation. For the Celebration of the Fiftieth Anniversary of the Reign of His Majesty the King of Saxony on 20 September 1818.) Autograph score. 1818. 14 leaves. 23.5 x 32.5 cm.
A: Title page
This festive orchestral work contains the melody "God Save the King" near the end.

162.
Morlacci, Francesco: Elegia (für Klavier). (Elegies for Piano.) Manuscript. Dresden, 1840. 2 leaves. 31.5 x 23.5 cm.
A: Pages 2–3
Only known piano composition by the last Italian court musical director.

163.
Becker, Wilhelm Gottlieb: Das Seifersdorfer Tal. (The Seifersdorf Valley.) Dresden, 1792. 176 pages, 4 leaves. 26 x 20 cm.
A: Pages 18–19
Temple of the Muses, with a bust of the poet Wieland.

164.
Wieland, Christoph Martin: Oberon. Weimar, 1781. 311 pages. 18.5 x 11.5 cm.
A: Flyleaf
With dedicatory poem by Wieland (1733–1813) to Countess Christina von Brühl (1756–1816), creator of the Seifersdorf nature trail.

165.
Schlegel, August Wilhelm: Autograph translation of Shakespeare's *As You Like It.* c. 1805. 54 leaves. 23 x 18.5 cm.
A: Leaves 39b–40a
Part of the extensive written legacy left by Schlegel, the important poet and translator of the German Romantic movement.

166.
Athenaeum. Edited by August Wilhelm Schlegel and Friedrich Schlegel. Vol. 1. Berlin, 1798. iv, 177, 178 pages. 21 x 12.5 cm.
A: Title page
The journal of the early German Romantic movement.

167.
Novalis (Friedrich von Hardenberg): Schriften. (Works.) Edited by Friedrich Schlegel and Ludwig Tieck. Berlin, 1802. 2 vols. xii, 338 p.; 552 p. 15.5 x 10 cm.
A: Title page
Novalis (1772–1801) is the most significant poet of the German Romantic period.

168.
Phöbus. (Phoebus.) Edited by Heinrich von Kleist and A. H. Müller. Vol. 1. Dresden, 1808. First through twelfth numbers, with 7 plates. 23 x 19 cm.
A: Title page and frontispiece (February).
A Dresden journal of the Romantic period.

169.
Königstein, Pfaffenstein, and Lilienstein Fortresses. c. 1825. Hand-colored etching. 48 x 63 cm.
This area, with its unique landscape, is situated along the Elbe River near Dresden.

170.
Meissen. View with the Elbe Bridge and the Albrecht Castle. 1808. Hand-colored etching. 58 x 69 cm.
Secular and religious center of the margraviate of Meissen during the Middle Ages and world-renowned center for the manufacture of Meissen porcelain.

171.
Portrait of Arthur Schopenhauer (1788–1860). 1855. Lithograph. 40 x 32.5 cm.
This great, if enigmatic, German philosopher later influenced Nietzche and Freud.

172.
Schopenhauer, Arthur: Die Welt als Wille und Vorstellung. (The World as Will and Idea.) Leipzig, 1819. 725 pages. 19.5 x 11.5 cm.
A: Title page.
The most important work by the eminent German philosopher written during his stay in Dresden.

173.
Graenicher, J. A.: Kostüme in Sachsen. (Traditional Dress in Saxony.) c. 1805. 18 plates, 5 leaves. 32 x 22 cm.
A: Plate 7
Depiction of a Wendish peasant in festive dress, a member of a Slavic minority that still lives in Saxony.

174. *See figure 36.*
Family Album of Johann Gottlieb Schwender. 1795–1810. 134 leaves. 12.5 x 22 cm.
A: Leaves 56b–57a
View of Dresden from the Elbe Bridge.

175.
Family Album of Wilhelm Ferdinand Teich. Dresden, 1809–24. 776 leaves. 11.5 x 40 cm.
A: Leaves 30b–31a, watercolor and script
Keeping Stammbücher *(family albums), customary since the sixteenth century, became very common around 1800 as an expression of the cult of friendship.*

176. *See figure 37.*
ROST, G. E.: Trachten der Berg- und Hüttenleute im Königreich Sachsen. (Traditional Dress of the Mining and Metallurgical Workers in the Kingdom of Saxony.) c. 1830. 2 leaves, colored engravings. 39 x 31 cm.
A: Leaves 176a–176b
Life and costumes of mine workers.

177.
Dresden. View from the South. c. 1820. Colored engraving. 43 x 56 cm.

178. *See figure 38.*
SCHUMANN, ROBERT: Des Sennen Abschied. (Senn's Farewell.) Lyrics by Friedrich Schiller. No. 22 from *Songs for the Young,* Opus 79. Autograph. Dresden, undated. 1 leaf. 27 x 19.5 cm.
A testimony to Schumann's creativity but also a historical account.

179. *See figure 39.*
BRAHMS, JOHANNES: *An ein Veilchen. Text von Ludwig Hölty. Lied für eine Singstimme und Klavier,* op. 49,2. (*To a Violet. Lyrics by Ludwig Hölty. Song for Voice and Piano,* opus 49.2.) Autograph fair copy. Before 1872. 2 leaves. 21.5 x 29 cm.
From a personal album kept by the Schumann family.

180.
RICHTER, ADRIAN LUDWIG: Autograph Letter to Hugo Bürkner. Loschwitz, 4 July 1864. 2 leaves, wrapper. 22 x 14.5 cm.
Richter (1803–84), who lived most of his life in Dresden, was an important German Romantic painter.

181.
RICHTER, ADRIAN LUDWIG: Der Sonntag in Bildern. (Sunday in Pictures.) Dresden, 1861. 10 plates. 35 x 27.5 cm.
A: "Visit to the Country"

From Faraway Lands

182. *See figure 40.*
Falnameh. Persia. Late sixteenth century. 103 pages. 68 x 51 cm.
A: Pages 73–74
"Muhammad splits the moon."

183.
Prayer to the Angels Fanuel and Michael. Ethiopia, eighteenth century. Vellum scroll. 40 x 13 cm.
Ethiopian prayer scroll.

184.
Tarba-Tzimbo. Kalmuck manuscript. Eighteenth century. 105 leaves. 42 x 16.5 cm.
Copy of a Buddhist manuscript.

185.
Buddhist Legends. Japan, nineteenth century. 24 leaves. 23.5 x 17.5 cm.
Manuscript in the Hiragana syllabary.

186.
Palmleaf Book. Java. 65 leaves. 25 x 43 cm.
Inscribed palm leaf and root.

187.
Astrological Almanach. China, nineteenth century. 59 leaves. 20.5 x 22 cm.
"The standard work fit for a hundred purposes."

188.
After Zacharais Wehme. A Portrait of Elector Augustus. 1586. Oil on canvas.
A copy from the end of the nineteenth century of an original portrait of 1586, by Zacharais Wehme (1558–1606).

189.
THEOBALD VON OËR: Winckelmann in der Nöthnitzer Bibliothek. (Winckelmann in the Nöthnitz Library.) 1874. Oil on canvas.
An idealized group portrait, showing the archaeologist-art historian Johann Winckelmann discoursing on an antique head before a group of great figures such as Lessing and Canaletto, 1874. Depicted are Winckelmann's friends and contemporaries, who were never together in Nöthnitz. From left to right: Archinto, Bünau, Francke, Algarotti, Rabener, Lessing, Winckelmann, Hagedorn, Oeser, Heyne, Lippert, Canaletto, and Dietrich.